God's Providence in Nature

Theological Reflections on Nature's Ecosystem and our Responsibilities

God's Providence in Nature

Theological Reflections on Nature's Ecosystem and our Responsibilities

Salai Hla Aung

2011

God's Providence in Nature: *Theological Reflections on Nature's Ecosystem and our Responsibilities* — Published by the Rev. Dr. Ashish Amos of the Indian Society for Promoting Christian Knowledge (ISPCK), Post Box 1585, 1654, Madarsa Road, Kashmere Gate, Delhi-110006.

© Author, 2011

ISBN: 978-81-8465-177-5

Laser typeset by

ISPCK, Post Box 1585, 1654, Madarsa Road, Kashmere Gate, Delhi-110006
• *Tel:* 23866323/22

e-mail: ashish@ispck.org.in • ella@ispck.org.in
website: www.ispck.org.in

Contents

Chapter VI   Concluding Observations

Preface

Experience is what matters most for life in this world. We are what we are through the formative influences of our various experiences in life. Experiences are the fundamental raw materials out of which one's personality is constituted. In other words, one's understanding of life and worldview are greatly influenced by one's life experiences. This connection has had very deep implications for me.

The manifold character of life experiences often causes problem for many. It creates confusion and conflict in one's inner life that continues to exist in until death. As a human being, I am no exception to this rule. I was brought up in a Christian family and am the youngest of the five siblings. I was fortunate to be the youngest because I am loved by all my brothers and sisters, and I continue to get support from them in many ways. My father was a Captain in the Army and retired from service in 1960. He was not so serious with religious observance; he was, however, a good Christian until his death in 1994. My mother is an ordinary housewife. Unlike my father she is a pious and devoted believer. She always tells us that her greatest desire for her children is that one of them becomes a full-time minister. It was due to her insistence that I decided to study theology. Regarding my education, I studied at the Rangoon University of Arts & Sciences and majored in Zoology. This course of study introduced me to evolutionary theory and all the scientific evidence in support of it. This apparent contradiction of my beliefs caused me spiritual confusion and conflict. Despite this inner turmoil, I decided to study theology at the Burma Institute of Theology (now changed to Myanmar Institute of Theology) and got a Master of Divinity degree in 1987.

What is already clear in my biographical story is the differences between my experiences at home and at school. At times they are sharply contradictory to each other. As a Christian, what I learned and experienced at home were mainly those things that pertain to the Christian faith and worldview; as a graduate in science, on the other hand, what I experienced were those things pertaining to science and the scientific worldview. This contradiction continues to cause confusion and conflict in my life. The scientific studies I undertook continue to have a powerful bearing on my understanding of life and the world. But so, too, do the cultural and spiritual norms of my tribe and my faith. I cannot judge for myself as to which of the two is of more fundamental import. I later overcame this conflict when I went to Germany to do my doctoral study. I was blessed at this juncture in the guidance of Prof. Dr. Hans Schwarz, who has marked interest in the dialogue between science and theology. He is a well-informed scholar as well as prolific writer. His book *Creation* (Grand Rapids, Michigan: William B. Eerdmans, 2002) and the dissertation of his American student, Mark William Worthing, which was later published under the rubric *God, Creation, and Contemporary Physics* by Fortress Press in the US in 1996 and won a Templeton Award, both bear witness to Prof. Schwarz's scholarship and contribution in the ongoing science/theology dialogue. His emphasis on this topic continues to prove very useful for me, because his lectures and literary works provide answers to many of the questions that cause my confusion. I acknowledge that this present work is a fruit of my doctoral study with him, for he awakened my interest in ecological issues and how they relate to the doctrine of creation.

The ecological crisis is truly a global crisis, and thus every nation faces the threat of its consequences in one way or another. Myanmar is no exception. Ecologically-related natural disasters like drought, flood, storms, landslides, etc., and their concomitant economic hardship catches everyone's attention. This environmentally-related misery is rather severe for the people of Myanmar: as a poor and developing country, it is inadequately prepared to cope with such calamitous events. Just as the present crisis affects every nation, so, too, it is the product of every nation's carelessness. Every society and nation on this earth bears some responsibility. All have contributed in one way or another. For instance, the ever-growing population in developing countries contributes its share to the mix. To meet the need of the growing population, forests and jungles are cleared for farmland and to make furniture. More and more trees are cut for wood year after year. Greater quantities of coal are burnt to meet the growing power supply. Toxic waste is carelessly produced and dumped without discrimination. All this abuse places a heavy burden on the ecosystem. The environment becomes more contaminated through the increased waste materials and living needs of the growing population. This direct link between the earth's growing population and the ecological crisis becomes an important question to be taken seriously, both theologically and ecclesiastically. As a professor of theology, I often discuss this question with my students and with the church elders because I want to increase their awareness. There will have to be a global movement if we are to deal successfully with the present crisis. Unless everyone is aware of the severity of the crisis and participates conscientiously in countering it, efforts will prove fruitless. Ultimately, we all have the obligation to take care of nature's wellbeing.

Science in the postmodern era is able to study the nature of reality in minute detail. The discoveries and postulations of postmodern science have had profound implications for faith. As Sir Karl Popper's proposition of falsification theory hints, many past scientific theories are now called into question and remain in need of reformulation in light of the conceptual implications of recent discoveries. Einstein's Theory of Relativity, for example, redefines the Newtonian understanding of gravity. The same is true with the reproduction of life. The successful cloning of Dolly the Sheep in Scotland a few years ago made everyone ponder again the mysterious wonder of reproduction. Such developments in postmodern science can have positive implications for faith: they open up new possibilities to talk meaningfully about God and His bountiful providence in nature for the wellbeing of all. The demonstration of this profuse providence in nature and its implications for ecological balance is the main focus of this work.

There are many to whom I owe thanks, and I must admit that I would never have been able to finish this book without their help and support. My thanks and gratitude go first to my former professor, Professor Hans Schwarz at Regensburg University in Germany. I owe him immensely for the precious advice and comments he has given to me concerning the work and also for his help in getting the work published. My gratitude goes also to Professor Gerald J. Pillay, Rector at Liverpool Hope University College in Liverpool, England, for his invitation to conduct research at Hope. I am also very much indebted to Olle Christoffersson, Agneta and Ivan Magnusson, the Baptist Union of Sweden, and the Stockholm School of Theology for their help in securing my visa to go to Sweden to continue the research, and also for the support they gave me during my sojourn there. I am especially thankful for Ulrich Dirlt and his family for their concern and support in many ways. I am immensely grateful for Robert Delaplane, Andy Metcalfe, Alice Rinell Hermansson, and Jennifer Endresen, who all helped in editing my language and improving the style. Many thanks go also to Frau Hildegard Ferme, secretary to Professor Hans Schwarz, for her help in preparing the book for publication. Prof. Schwarz's research assistant, Nathan Yoder, deserves a big thank you for carefully reading and amending the whole manuscript. Above all, I voice my love and gratitude to my wife, Sui Cer Ling, and our three children, Paul Martin, Zing Ttha Iang Par and Ca Ttha Hlei Par, for their constant support through prayer and willingness and patience in allowing me to remain abroad for such a long period of time. Needless to say, they are quite happy that I have completed this project.

Salai Hla Aung

Hakha (Chin State), Myanmar 2011

Chapter I

Some Facts as Seen with the Eyes of Faith

With regard to his personal impression about the deeper meaning and implication of the cosmos, the Japanese philosopher Yujiro Nakamura (b. 1925) refers to the insights of the French philosopher and scientist Blaise Pascal (1623-62) who exhibited a deep understanding of the natural world. Nakamura writes:

> Now, in relation to the notion of "cosmos," let me explain a passage I still remember from when I was young, and specialized in the study of Pascal. The passage is, "the infinite silence of this universe frightens me." This passage is very famous in describing his fear of the cosmos, which to him was the dwelling place of the divine or a place full of meaning, and a vast open space which in Cartesian physical terms was called the cosmos.[1]

For a devout person like Blaise Pascal, the universe or the world would still symbolize the glory of God and is full of meaning with regard to life here on earth. Modern scientific surveys and portraits of the world give support to at least the second part of Pascal's view, i.e., the world as a place full of meaning. One can see this in the way the world is structured and how all its parts are related to each other structurally and functionally. More elaboration will follow in the coming discussion.

---

[1] Yujiro Nakamura, "The Resonance of the Cosmos," in *Cosmos " Life " Religion: Beyond Humanism* (Tenri: Tenri University Press, 1988), 378.

1.1   The Planet Earth in the Universe

The planet earth, as all are well familiar, is one of the planets in the solar system. The solar system finds itself in the constellation of stars called the Milky Way Galaxy. There are several billion stars and their corresponding planets in the Milky Way. The star in this solar system, i.e., the Sun, is only one of the several billion stars in the Milky Way Galaxy.[2] The Milky Way itself is only one of the galaxies in the galactic group called "The Local Group", which is made up of about 32 small galaxies.[3] Although there are several different estimations among scientists concerning the diameter of the visible universe, the most conservative estimation is about 15 billion light years.[4] This is only a rough estimation, though, and no one can say exactly how big and how vast the universe really is.[5] Across this 15-billion-light-year diameter of the universe there exist several billion galaxies.[6]

The position of the planet earth within the solar system is amazingly well-placed; i.e., in a way that makes the emergence and continuation of life on earth possible.[7] The earth is situated at a distance of about 150 million kilometers away from the sun. The position of the earth at this distance from the sun helps it avoid becoming either too hot or too cold. If the earth were moved within the orbit of Venus, then it would become

---

[2] Stephen Hawking, *The Universe in a Nutshell* (London: Bantam Press, 2001), 69.

[3] *The Heavens: The World Book Encyclopedia of Science*, vol. 1 (Chicago: World Book, Inc., 1992), 74.

[4] John D. Barrow, *Theories of Everything: The Quest for Ultimate Explanation* (Oxford: Clarendon Press, 1991), 132. 15 billion light years implies the time needed for light to travel across the universe from one end to the other. In a vacuum light travels at the speed of 186,000 miles per second. One can figure out how vast the universe is from a combination of the speed of light and the light years. Lineweaver and Davis have recently calculated the radius of the universe to be more than 14 billion light years due to its continuous expansion, Charles H. Lineweaver and Tamara M. Davis, "Misconceptions about the Big Bang," in *Scientific American*, vol. 292, No. 3 (March 2005), 32.

[5] Stephen Hawking, *A Brief History of Time: From the Big Bang to Black Holes* (London: Bantam Press, 1988), 136.

[6] Stephen Hawking, *The Universe in a Nutshell*, 69.

[7] Cf. *The Planet Earth: The World Book Encyclopedia of Science*, vol. 4, 14.

unpleasantly hot, as Venus is about 42 million kilometers closer to the sun.[8] Being closer to the sun, the temperature of the earth's atmosphere would rise until its limestone deposits disintegrate and release carbon dioxide. Large amounts of this greenhouse gas would then pour into the atmosphere. The result would be a condition totally inhospitable for life.[9] If the earth, on the other hand, were moved within the orbit of Mars, then it would enter into a cataclysmic ice age, for Mars lies 78 million kilometers further away from the sun and therefore receives considerably less heat.[10] In such a situation the earth's oceans would freeze, and consequently the water content in the atmosphere would decrease dramatically. This would forever change the earth into an environment inhospitable for life.[11]

The size of the planet earth is big enough (i.e., its gravity is strong enough) to retain an atmosphere which is dense enough and has the right composition to form a pleasant greenhouse blanket. Had the size of the planet earth been only the size of the moon, its gravity would be much reduced, and thus it would have a problem in retaining its atmosphere. As a result, the air would start to get thinner as the gas molecules of the atmosphere leave the planet. The ocean would release its own gas content, and then it too would slowly evaporate in an attempt to replenish the atmosphere. The atmospheric gaseous molecules would escape into space until the ocean was exhausted entirely.[12] It is interesting, however, that it is only the planet earth that has such a life-supporting atmosphere among the planets in the solar system. This unique distinction deserves a closer examination: how exactly does the atmosphere protect and nurture life?

---

[8] For exact information about the distances of planets from the sun see the discussion in the conclusion section.

[9] Cf. Francis Crick, *Life Itself: Its Origin and Nature* (London: MacDonald & Co., 1981), 102.

[10] About the distances of planets from the sun, see the discussion in the conclusion section.

[11] Cf. Francis Crick, *Life Itself*, 102ff.

[12] Cf. Hugh Ross, "Astronomical Evidences for a Personal, Transcendent God," in *The Creation Hypothesis: Scientific Evidence for Intelligent Design*, ed. J. P. Moreland (Downers Grove, Illinois: InterVarsity Press, 1994), 166.

1.2   Atmospheric Structure

Generally speaking, the earth's atmosphere is basically made up of four different layers: troposphere, stratosphere, mesosphere and thermosphere.[13] The layer nearest to the earth is called "troposphere" (literally, "the turning or changing sphere") and extends 8 to 10 kilometers high.[14] Eighty percent of the atmospheric mass occurs in this sphere,[15] and thus most of the weather (such as rain, snow and clouds) takes place in this region due to its high density of atmospheric composition. In other words, this region is predominantly characterized by changes and turnings of air, which is responsible for weather formation and pattern. The next layer is called the stratosphere ("the layered sphere") and extends upward to 50 kilometers.[16] This section of the atmosphere is important because in its upper regions lies the so-called ozone layer which absorbs the ultraviolet radiation from the sun. Ninety-nine percent of the atmospheric mass is located in the troposphere and stratosphere – below 30 km, to be exact.[17] Because of the relatively massive concentration of greenhouse gases such as CO_2, O_3, methane, and water vapor, and the longer residing time of aerosol in the troposphere and stratosphere, the phenomena leading to global warming originate in this part of the atmosphere. The layer above the stratosphere is called the mesosphere ("middle sphere"; hence the middle atmosphere). It is just above the stratosphere and extends to 80 kilometers high.[18] Temperatures here fall as low as -93 degrees Celsius. The deep temperature in this region helps the water vapor in the lower atmosphere form clouds. Without cloud formation, the life-supporting weather system is hardly conceivable. Beyond the mesosphere is the thermosphere (also known as the upper atmosphere). It extends

---

[13] The exosphere is usually included in the earth's atmosphere in detailed discussion about atmospheric science.

[14] *The Planet Earth: The World Book Encyclopedia of Science*, 26.

[15] John M. Wallace and Peter V. Hobbs, *Atmospheric Science: An Introductory Survey* (New York: Academic Press, 1977), 22.

[16] *The Planet Earth: The World Book Encyclopedia of Science*, 26.

[17] John T. Houghton, *The Physics of Atmosphere* (Cambridge: Cambridge University Press, 1986), 57f.

[18] *The Planet Earth: The World Book Encyclopedia of Science*, 26.

approximately up to 500 kilometers high.[19] Temperatures here rise as altitude increases due to heightened absorption of solar radiation and can reach as high as 1,727 degrees Celsius.[20] Accordingly, strong photo-dissociation occurs here.[21] The high temperature in this region also serves as a protective shield against the intruding attacks of meteorites from outer space by burning them up.[22] If most of the meteorites entering earth's atmosphere were not destroyed in this region, the earth would experience natural catastrophes quite often – which, needless to say, would have extremely negative consequences for life.[23] Moreover, this would likely pose big challenges in the development of modern aerospace industry. Aircraft in the sky could be struck by intruding meteorites, resulting in a widespread fear of air travel.[24]

This thermosphere is also known as "ionosphere" because of the ionization process that occurs here. The sun's energy is so strong in this region that it breaks apart molecules and atoms of air, leaving ions (i.e., atoms with missing electrons) and free-floating electrons. The large number of free electrons in the ionosphere allows for the transmission of electromagnetic waves. Radio signals " a form of electromagnetic waves " are reflected by the ionosphere and make radio communication possible over long distances.[25] The existence of charged particles in this region gives rise to a potential electro-sphere, which together with earth's magnetosphere acts as a protective shield from the lethal attacks of solar

---

[19] *The Planet Earth: The World Book Encyclopedia of Science*, 26.

[20] The high temperature in this region must be seen in terms of kinetic theory. This means the temperature is carried within the moving individual atoms.

[21] *Encyclopedia Britannica*, vol. 2 (Chicago: Encyclopaedia Britanniaca Inc.), 309.

[22] See *McGraw-Hill Encyclopedia of Science & Technology*, vol. 11 (New York: McGraw-Hill, 2002), 1. The disintegration of intruding objects from outer space in the upper sky is observed as "shooting" or "falling stars" from the earth's surface, Cf. *The Hutchison Concise Encyclopedia* (London: BCA, 1994), 595.

[23] Cf. Clark R. Chapman, "Comet on Target for Jupiter," in *Nature* vol. 363, 10 June (1993), 492.

[24] Planes usually fly in the stratosphere.

[25] J. M. Wallace and P. V. Hobbs, *Atmospheric Science*, 16f.

storms.[26] These "storms" are winds of electrically charged particles coming from the sun with a very high speed, about 300 to 500 kilometers (i.e., 186 to 311 miles) per second.[27] If the solar winds are not repelled by the earth's magnetosphere, the possibility of aviation is highly questionable.

What is of special interest in the atmospheric phenomena is the way the air is dissipated and mixed uniformly across the atmosphere as a whole. The natural mechanism that drives these phenomena is rather fascinating, too. Gases of different molecular weights tend to separate from each other.[28] This tendency, however, is naturally prevented by atmospheric motions such as turbulence, atmospheric winds, etc. These natural phenomena dissipate and mix the principal atmospheric gases uniformly, thereby creating the necessary conditions for our weather system. If this natural mechanism did not exist, earth's weather would be really chaotic, probably transforming the planet into a place unfit for life. The earth's fine and conducive weather system is therefore a direct result of this uniform dissipation and mixture of gases across the vast atmosphere.

In light of the above discussion, the ecological implications and significance of the massive concentration of major atmospheric gaseous constituents become apparent. Only in recent history have people come to learn the importance of the massive concentration of those constituents. Even as late as the 16th century, people still believed that the atmosphere was weightless.[29] This enormous concentration of gases gives mass, weight, and density to the atmosphere, thereby making the formation and movement of turbulence, wind, and other atmospheric flows possible. The following figures show exactly how massive and dense the atmosphere

---

[26] *Ibid.*, 18-21. For a greater-detailed scientific explanation about this with pictorial illustration, see *McGraw-Hill Encyclopedia of Science & Technology*, vol. 10, 331f.

[27] *Encyclopedia Britannica*, vol. 6, 27.

[28] *Ibid.*, vol. 2, 309.

[29] *Ibid.*, vol. 6, 81.

[30] *The Planet Earth: The World Book Encyclopedia of Science*, vol. 4, 142.

is.[30]

Gas	% by Volume	Weight (Kilograms)
Nitrogen	78.09	3,840,000,000
Oxygen	20.95	11,800,000
Argon[31]	0.93	-
Carbon Dioxide	0.033	2,600,000
Neon	0.0018	64,000
Helium	0.00052	3,700
Methane	0.00015	4,300
Krypton	0.0001	15,000
Nitrous Oxide	0.00005	4,000
Hydrogen	0.00005	180
Ozone	0.00004	3,100
Xenon	0.000008	180

The impact of gravitational force upon the voluminous mass of these gases gives rise to atmospheric pressure, and the temperature differential further gives rise to differences in the atmospheric pressure. This pressure differential, in turn, causes turbulence, winds, and other atmospheric flows. All this has made the weather system suitable for life on earth. One can see clearly how miraculously the natural system works. The most abundant

---

[31] The weight of Argon is not provided in the referred source. In the calculation of Wallace and Hobbs the ratio of Nitrogen, Oxygen, and Argon by mass is 75.51%, 23.14% and 1.28% respectively. If one is to estimate the weight of Argon on the basis of this calculation, it would then be slightly in excess of the combined weight of the remaining gaseous constituents. For the full report of Wallace and Hobbs, see their *Atmospheric Science*, 5.

and massive constituent of the atmosphere, viz., nitrogen, is a non-greenhouse gas, and a not-so-reactive gas as well.[32] Because of this property, atmospheric nitrogen concentration helps the atmosphere retain a stable and reliable density without causing any harmful consequence for the natural system.[33] If nitrogen reacted strongly with other gases, as other greenhouse gases are prone to do, then the earth would probably not have a stable and congenial climate. Instead, the planet would have the kind of weather which is rather uncongenial and unstable. Once again, the outcome would mean a chaotic situation for life here on earth.

All these facts show that the vast extension of the atmosphere enables it to provide a protective as well as nurturing environment for life on earth. The immense atmospheric envelope helps the earth to balance its ecosystem. It also provides enough space for the regulation of temperatures and weather on earth through the formation of clouds and precipitation. One should give thanks to God for providing such a vast and thick atmosphere, making life enjoyable, comfortable, and prosperous. The ozone layer in the atmosphere is worthy of special attention, for it is a prime example of how the protective system of nature works for life.

1.3 Enclosure of the Earth Surface by the Ozone Layer

It is a well-known fact that the earth is blanketed by a thin layer of gas called ozone. Ozone is a chemical compound whose molecule is composed of three oxygen atoms. The existence of an ozone layer in the stratosphere is so beneficial to life here on earth because it strongly absorbs the ultraviolet rays from the sun, which are very harmful to health, be it human or otherwise. The ultraviolet radiation can cause skin cancer and damages

---

[32] For more information about the atmospheric reactive gases other than the common greenhouse gases and ozone depleting gases, see *Climate Change 2001: The Scientific Basis: Contribution of Working Group I to the Third Assessment Report of the Intergovernmental Panel on Climate Change*, ed. J. T. Houghton (New York: Cambridge University Press, 2001), 256-260. Hereafter will be abbreviated as Intergovernmental Panel on Climate Change 2001.

[33] Cf. Hugh Montefiore, *The Probability of God* (London: SCM Press Ltd., 1985), 48.

to vegetation, among other things.

The ozone layer is scattered between 44 and 56 kilometers up in the atmosphere, i.e., in the upper end of the stratosphere.[34] Ozone is formed when highly energetic solar radiation strikes molecules of oxygen (O_2) and causes the two Oxygen atoms to split apart. This process is known as photodissociation. The free oxygen atom reacts with another oxygen molecule and forms ozone (O_3). This process is known as photolysis. Ozone dissolves again naturally by absorbing ultraviolet radiation from the sun and also by a chemical reaction with various compounds containing nitrogen, hydrogen, and chlorine. These chemicals all occur naturally in the atmosphere in very small amounts.

In an unperturbed atmosphere there is a balance between the amount of ozone being produced and the amount of ozone being destroyed. As a result, the total amount of ozone in the stratosphere remains relatively constant. In recent decades, however, this natural balance of ozone in the atmosphere has been perturbed by anthropogenic production and emission of ozone-depleting chemicals. The production and emission of these chemicals grew rapidly, and the gradual erosion of the ozone layer intensified to the point that several holes in the ozone layer have occurred in the last few years.[35] The following chart shows the presence and concentration of those ozone-depleting substances in the atmosphere between the pre-industrial era and the present.[36]

---

[34] *The Planet Earth: The World Book Encyclopedia of Science*, 23.

[35] The destruction rate of the ozone layer was so alarming that world leaders gathered together and made an agreement in Montreal, Canada, to prevent the situation from becoming uncontrollable by reducing the production of chemicals that deplete ozone in half by 2000. See Joel L. Swerdlow, "Making Sense of the Millennium," in *National Geographic*, vol. 193, No. 1 (January 1998), 5. This agreement is called the Montreal Protocol. It was first adopted in 1987 and subsequently adjusted and amended in London (1990), Copenhagen (1992), Vienna (1995), Montreal (1997), and Beijing (1999). The main goal of the protocol is to control the consumption and production of chlorine- and bromine-containing chemicals such as CFCs, methyl chloroform, carbon tetrachloride, and many others that destroy stratospheric ozone. See *Intergovernmental Panel on Climate Change 2001*, 794.

[36] *Ibid.*, 358.

Gas	Abundance (Year 1750)	Abundance (Year 1998)	Radiative Forcing (Wm^{-2})
CH_4	700	1745	0.48
N_2O	270	314	0.15
CFC-11	0	268	0.07
CFC-12	0	533	0.17
CFC-13	0	4	0.001
CFC-113	0	84	0.03
CFC-114	0	15	0.005
CFC-115	0	7	0.001
CCL4	0	102	0.01
CH_3CCL_3	0	69	0.004
HCFC-22	0	132	0.03
HCFC-141b	0	10	0.001
HCFC-142b	0	11	0.002
Halon-1211	0	3.8	0.001
Halon-1301	0	2.5	0.001

Note: The concentration rate of CH_4 and N_2O is in parts per billion (ppb), and for other gases is in parts per trillion (ppt).

The total absence of many of the ozone-depleting gases in the pre-industrial time clearly indicates that human activities are the main cause for the

---

[37] These gases also act as greenhouse gases. The formation of the ozone holes is an indirect indicator of the gases' capacity for radiation emission.

occurrence of these ozone holes.[37] It now becomes clear from measurements in the polar firn air, i.e., the air enclosed in polar ice, that there are no natural sources for those chemical compounds.[38] The most destructive among them are the so-called chlorofluorocarbons (CFCs). Scientists first observed the destructive effect of the CFCs on the ozone layer in the 1970s.[39] The CFCs were invented in the 1930s and used widely in refrigeration and electronic industries. It is found that one chlorine atom from a CFC can destroy more than 100,000 ozone molecules.[40] This means that human activities have a profound implication for the state of ozone in the atmosphere. According to the report of the Intergovernmental Panel on Climate Change, the future state of the ozone layer depends upon the following three factors:

1.   The magnitude of future consumption of ozone-depleting substances by developing countries.

2.   The projected abundance of CH_4 and N_2O.

3.   The projected climate change impacts on stratospheric temperatures and circulation.[41]

Due to the conscientious implementation of the international Montreal Protocol, the ozone condition in the atmosphere has now recovered to a substantially more preferable level.[42] But this does not mean that the danger has gone away forever. The potential for harm still lingers on, and it could worsen immediately if many nations do not abide by the Montreal Protocol and resume their production of ozone-depleting chemical substances. Thus, countries ought to be on guard against this abuse by giving serious consideration to this issue in their interior policy making. By conscientiously sticking to the Montreal Protocol, the world's nations enhance the chances for the survival of the human race and at the same time prepare good, healthy, and pleasant living environments for future

---

[38] Cf. *Intergovernmental Panel on Climate Change 2001*, 255.

[39] Cf. Joel L. Swerdlow," Making Sense of the Millennium," 5.

[40] *Ibid.*

[41] Cf. *Intergovernmental Panel on Climate Change 2001*, 256.

[42] *Ibid.*

generations. This problem is a most urgent moral challenge, an existential obligation that every individual person and nation should take seriously.

While the earth's atmosphere has major providential significance and ecological implications, the oceans are no less wondrous. The next section will focus on the providential role the seas play in nature's life-supporting ecosystem.

1.4   70% Coverage of the Earth by Water

It is frankly amazing that while fully 70% of the earth's surface is covered by water, there are no findings to suggest an abundance of water in any of its three forms (solid, fluid, and vapor) on the surface of other nearby planets.[43] That the earth could not become a good habitat for a wide variety of living organisms without such a huge volume of water is scientifically indisputable. The enormous size of the seas and oceans combined naturally arouses curiosity in many people and poses the question: where does all this water come from, anyway? Scientists assume that the water in the seas and oceans, as well as the gases in the atmosphere, are produced by volcanic eruptions.[44] They believe that when much of the huge amount of gases released into the atmosphere by volcanoes got cooled, water was formed, and the seas and oceans subsequently emerged. A brief digression is necessary at this juncture in order to discuss the inner formation of the earth and its providential implications and significance for life.

The innermost core of the earth is a fiery, burning region with temperatures reaching up to 5000 degrees Celsius.[45] Because of both these extreme inner core temperatures and the relatively high temperature in the outer core (i.e., between 2200 and 5000 degrees Celsius), iron and nickel, comprising the main components of the earth's core, melt. An electrical

---

[43] This 70% coverage of the earth by water includes only the liquid form. It does not include the snow and ice of the polar regions or the water vapor in the atmosphere.

[44] Cf. John M. Wallace and Peter V. Hobbs, *Atmospheric Science*, 4.

[45] *The Planet Earth: The World Book Encyclopedia of Science*, 48.

[46] Cf. Gary A. Glatzmaier and Peter Olson, "Probing the Geodynamo," in *Scientific American*, vol. 292, No. 4 (April 2005), 34f.

current system caused by the flow of electrically charged particles emerges in this melting region.[46] These electrical currents produce a magnetic field that passes through the flowing liquid and generates more electric currents. This reinforces the original current in a self-exciting manner.[47] The result is the magnetic field of the earth, also known as the geomagnetic field. Fully 95% of the earth's magnetic force stems from these marvelous natural phenomena inside the earth's core.[48] The implication and significance of this geomagnetic field for human well-being is profound. The presence of magnetic forces makes possible the use of the compass for navigation, thereby allowing for a maximization of economic and cultural advantages. If this geomagnetic field were not in existence, the consequences would be disastrous. Explorers throughout history would have faced overwhelming difficulty in traveling across oceans. For the European peoples, especially, the migration to the New World would have posed enormous difficulty, and the resulting cultural consequences would have been enormous. Europeans would likely have been stuck within the confines of their continent, their ever-growing population exerting greater pressure on the various nations as arable and habitable land, so essential for survival and prosperity, proportionately decreased. This would have caused nations to make war against each other, draining much of their resources, both human and material. A heavy check on economic development and progress would have occurred; indeed, it is almost impossible to speculate whether human civilization would have come to the present stage, since modern technology originated in Europe.

The salinity of ocean water also contributes much to the ecological welfare of the earth. Ocean water contains about 3 to 3.4% of salt. If the seas contained more salt or a higher salinity, the rate of evaporation would differ sharply from the present rate: it would increase substantially, as is the case in the Mediterranean and Dead Sea.[49] It is difficult to calculate precisely the kind of impact of such a high evaporation rate upon the ecosystem of the earth. What one can say for sure, however, is that it would

---

[47] Self-exciting dynamos can be made in the laboratory experimentally. See *The Planet Earth: The World Book Encyclopedia of Science*, vol. 4, 17.

[48] Cf. *Encyclopedia Britannica*, vol. 6, 27.

[49] *Ibid.*, vol. 13, 487f.

be significant. The most easily calculable outcome of this high evaporation rate would be a higher concentration of water vapor in the atmosphere. This would probably increase the absorption and reemission of the reflected radiation from the earth's surface, and the temperature would rise accordingly.[50] It could eventually lead to increased rainfall and frequent flooding. The ecological consequences of lower salinity could also be great. Lower salinity would probably impact the inner ocean currents. The seawater would become less dense; this could lead to a vertical stratification in the sink region, which in turn would have a bearing upon the transportation of dissolved CO_2 from the sink regions to the source regions through the inner ocean currents.[51] A slower evaporation rate could also cause other problems, such as drought, lesser rainfall, cloud formation, etc. All this indicates that any change in the salinity of ocean water and the corresponding change in evaporation rate would not be beneficial for the ecosystem.

The worst consequence of higher salinity would be its effect upon marine biology. Seas and oceans are home to countless forms of plant and animal life. The ecological benefits of these sea plants and organisms through their physiological and biological activities have not yet been adequately assessed. Research indicates that if the salinity of ocean water rises to the point of 6%, many of those sea plants and organisms could not survive or flourish.[52]

Even though more salt has been steadily added into the oceans from terrestrial runoff in huge amounts annually, the salinity of the seas and oceans remains constant; how is this possible? The scientific explanation about the mechanisms that keep the salinity of ocean water constant is nothing short of amazing. Among the countless organisms in the oceans are the coccolithopores, whose shells are made up of calcium carbonate,

---

[50] Water is second only to CO_2 in terms of radiation forcing. See *Intergovernmental Panel on Climate Change 2001*, 358.

[51] Cf. *ibid.*, 200. Also see Anne Platt McGinn, "Safeguarding the Health of Oceans," in *Worldwatch Paper* 145 (Washington, D. C.: Worldwatch Institute, 1999), 16f.

[52] Cf. Hugh Montefiore, *The Probability of God*, 53.

and the diatoms, whose skeletal walls are made up of silica. Ninety-nine percent of the silica washed down by rivers into the sea sinks to the ocean floor. The number of the diatoms in the oceans is directly proportional to the content of the silica washed down by rivers.[53] The more silica entering the marine ecosystem, the greater the number of diatoms there are in the sea, and vice versa. The silica falling to the seabed together with other sinking debris simply traps the "alien" salt and removes it from the ocean.[54]

Another role which the oceans play in the ecosystem of the world is the balancing of CO_2 in the atmosphere. Scientists estimate that the oceans contain 50 times more CO_2 than the atmosphere.[55] Moreover, research reveals that about 70 to 80% of anthropogenic production of CO_2 has been absorbed by the oceans.[56] How big is the capacity of the oceans for the intake of CO_2? If the ocean did not have the capacity to incorporate such a large amount of CO_2, the climatic chaos caused by the excessive CO_2 levels in the atmosphere due to human production would be unimaginable. This fact should not, however, be taken to imply that the natural system has a fool-proof, inexhaustible capacity to adjust to adverse changes, thereby keeping the necessary conditions for life unhampered and unhindered. Scientific studies show that the ocean's capacity has a boundary, a limit that is dependent upon various factors; these include the degree of salinity, alkality, CO_2 concentration of ocean water, atmospheric CO_2 concentration, surface water temperature, pollution, etc.

It is undeniable that the salinity, CO_2 concentration of ocean water, surface water temperature, and pollution of the oceans are directly related to human activities. Heightened use of artificial fertilizers increases the salinity levels. All the industrial waste dumped into rivers eventually reaches the sea and pollutes the ocean water.[57] This pollution destroys not

---

[53] *Ibid.*, 54.

[54] *Ibid.*

[55] Cf. *Intergovernmental Panel on Climate Change 2001*, 197.

[56] *Ibid.*, 199. This 70-to-80% is meant only for anthropogenic emissions. The anthropogenic emission of CO_2 accounts for about half of the total emission into the atmosphere. Other sources of emission are change of land use, forest fires, evapotranspiration, etc. Cf. *ibid.*, 189-193.

[57] For more see Anne Platt McGinn, "Safeguarding the Health of Oceans."

only the habitats of the oceanic organisms but also many of the organisms themselves. The growing consumption of fossil fuels only adds more CO_2 into the atmosphere and the oceans as well. This in turn will trap more heat in the atmosphere, thereby increasing surface temperature. This relationship reveals that the increased anthropogenic production of CO_2 has immediate consequences for CO_2 concentration in ocean water and surface water temperature. At present, one cannot say exactly how things will develop, because the oceanic ecosystem has not yet been fully observed and scientifically surveyed in detail.[58] In any case, what one can say for sure is that the uncontrolled and unprotected anthropogenic production of CO_2 certainly has profound implications for the well-being of the marine ecosystem.

The oceanic absorption of atmospheric CO_2 is an amazing process. Chemically, CO_2 is strongly soluble in water, and most of the uptake of CO_2 by the oceans takes place through molecular diffusion across the air-sea interface. A net CO_2 transfer can take place whenever there is a partial pressure difference of CO_2 across the interface. This process is also known as flux, and it can be described as the joint product of a gas transfer coefficient, the solubility of CO_2, and the partial pressure difference of CO_2 between air and water.[59] Here we can see the logical significance of the 70% coverage of the earth's surface by water. The vast surface of the oceans increases the degree of interface between air and water, thereby creating a natural mechanism to absorb more of the CO_2 from the atmosphere. The atmospheric content of CO_2 is balanced, and in this way the overheating of the earth due to high CO_2 concentration is naturally

---

[58] Cf. Yvonne Baskin, *The Work of Nature*, 197.

[59] Cf. *Intergovernmental Panel on Climate Change 2001*, 197.

[60] Because the land masses of the continents deflect the ocean currents, the ocean currents usually flow in a large circular path called *gyres*. The principal gyres move in a clockwise direction in the North Atlantic and North Pacific Oceans and anti-clockwise in the South Atlantic and South Pacific oceans due to the Coriolis effect. The North Atlantic gyre is composed of three major currents: the Gulf Stream, the Canary Current, and the North Equatorial Currents (see *The Planet Earth: The World Book Encyclopedia of Science*, 40). Heat transfer and

prevented. Because the solubility of CO_2 is inversely proportional to temperature, the ocean's capacity to absorb CO_2 is stronger in cool regions like the Northern hemisphere. The importance of ocean currents comes into play at this juncture.[60] Although CO_2 absorption is greater in cooler climates, there are no barriers between cool and warm regions when it comes to ocean circulation. CO_2 is thus dispersed effortlessly throughout the world's oceans by means of the current. What is of particular interest in this connection is that warm surface water temperature tends to increase the outflow of CO_2 from the oceans.[61] The process proceeds as follows: the warmer the atmospheric temperature is, the warmer the surface water temperature becomes and the greater the outgasing rate of CO_2 from the oceans is. What would happen if the outflow rate becomes greater than the absorption rate? The potential consequences are totally incalculable.

Countless phytoplanktons and zooplanktons in the oceans are also very effective natural mechanisms in balancing the CO_2 concentration in the atmosphere. Research indicates a net consumption of CO_2 by phytoplanktons through the photosynthesis process in the upper warm layer of the ocean water. One should note that phytoplanktons are naturally prosperous and numerous in coastal areas; about 14 to 30% of net CO_2 consumption by phytoplanktons occurs here.[62] The implication is that the pollution of ocean water matters a great deal: the greater the level of pollution, the more the phytoplanktons in the coastal areas would be harmed. The value of this natural mechanism of CO_2 balancing is vividly reflected by the scientific suggestion to "green" the ocean coastal areas in order to increase the uptake of CO_2 from the atmosphere. It is calculated that if all the world's coastal areas were seeded with green algae, it would consume much of the CO_2 in the atmosphere and could even solve the

---

CO_2 transfer between the warm and cool regions are due to the combined effect of the flows of these currents and deep ocean currents, which are caused by the differential in the salinity and temperature of the ocean waters. The deep ocean currents flow beneath warmer and less dense surface water. Cold water has greater salinity and is denser than warmer water, cf. *Ibid.*, 41.

[61] Cf. *Intergovernmental Panel on Climate Change 2001*, 197.

[62] Cf. *Ibid.*, 198.

[63] Yvonne Baskin, *The Work of Nature*, 197.

global warming due to the increased CO_2 concentration. Scientists carried out experiments by dripping diluted iron solution into several square kilometers of oceans and found that algae grow rapidly with a corresponding increased drawdown of CO_2.[63] This practice, however, is not without risk; scientists are simply unsure about the possible ecological consequences of fertilizing millions of square kilometers of ocean water with continuous doses of iron. Baskin clarifies the issue by her following argument:

> The notion of deliberately polluting the ocean to counter our unintentional pollution of the atmosphere leaves many deeply troubled – especially when human societies have made little attempt to tackle the underlying problem by reducing carbon emission at the source.[64]

The role of countless zooplanktons in the oceans in balancing CO_2 levels is also remarkable. The shells of many marine organisms are made up of solid calcium carbonate ($CaCO_3$). When the organisms die, the shells sink down and accumulate in sediments, such as coral reefs and sand. Fully 60% of the calcium carbonate in the shells of marine organisms eventually ends up in this fashion.[65] If put in numerical figures, the total $CaCO_3$ sediment accumulation comes to the amount of 0.7PgC/yr.[66] This figure shows that marine organisms play a significant role in the ecosystem of the earth; their well-being, however, is contingent upon the quality of seawater. Excessive pollution can destroy the organisms as well as many of the nutrients on which the organisms feed. For instance, nitrates from artificial fertilizers washed down into the ocean by runoff raises the salinity of sea water, thereby severely endangering many the marine organisms.[67] Other industrial wastes can cause danger in multiple ways. In other words, human attitude and behavior are essential when it comes to the health

---

[64] *Ibid.*

[65] Cf. *Intergovernmental Panel on Climate Change 2001*, 198.

[66] 1PgC is equal to 1GtC. One GtC is one gigaton of carbon, i.e., one billion tons. 0.7 PgC/yr would then mean a total of 700 million tons of carbon. Cf. *ibid.*, 198, 870.

[67] Hugh Montefiore, *The Probability of God*, 48.

and stability of an ecosystem.

Chemical reactions in seawater are yet another important way that the ocean balances the atmospheric content of CO_2. Ninety-one percent of seawater CO_2 subsists as bicarbonate ion (HCO_3^-), 8% as carbonate ion (CO_3^{2-}), and 1% as molecular CO_2.[68] Bicarbonate ions are produced through the reaction of carbon dioxide, water and carbonate ion. Since it is an ionized compound, the bicarbonate ion is chemically reactive – i.e., it can react with other dissolved chemical elements in the oceans and produce new compounds. While some of the products of these unions continue to subsist in the water in a dissolved form, the rest sink into the seabed as sediment. A certain amount of carbon dioxide is therefore kept apart from the natural cycle and stored in the ocean floor.[69] There is, however, a natural hindrance to this process. When the atmospheric CO_2 concentration is too high, the dissolved CO_2 content of seawater increases accordingly. This occurs because the CO_2 reacts with the carbonate ions to form bicarbonate ions.[70] Since the amount of carbonate ions is rather low, only a portion of the dissolved CO_2 is required to react with the carbonate ions; the rest remains as dissolved CO_2. The chemical chain reaction of CO_2 in ocean water is one of nature's effective mechanisms against human mismanagement, incorporating about 70 to 80% of the total anthropogenic CO_2.[71]

The key importance of ocean currents becomes apparent in light of the above discussion. The inner ocean currents regulate the earth's weather system by coupling with the atmosphere and by dissipating and mixing chemicals throughout the world's seas. As mentioned previously, the oceanic incorporation of atmospheric CO_2 is very much dependent upon the currents, for they transport the dissolved CO_2 from the sink (cool) regions to the source (warm) regions. These currents also serve in

---

[68] Cf. *Intergovernmental Panel on Climate Change 2001*, 197.

[69] Cf. *Ibid.*, 188f.

[70] *Ibid.*, 197.

[71] Cf. *McGraw-Hill Encyclopedia of Science & Technology*, vol. 2, 329f. Also Cf. J. R. Toggweiler, "Carbon Overconsumption," in *Nature*, vol. 363 (May 20, 1993), 210f.

distributing organic material evenly throughout the seas, and invaluable service to the countless phyto- and zooplanktons that subsist on nutrients replenished in this manner.

The environmental and ecological benevolence that water brings to the earth's ecosystem is utterly remarkable. The physical properties of water make it an ideal means for conditioning the climate on earth. It can store heat better than most other substances; this is the reason why we need time to heat water and why the hot water needs time to become cool again. Water takes up heat when it transforms itself from solid to fluid and fluid to vapor, and it releases heat when it transforms itself from vapor to fluid and fluid to solid. The latent heat stored in vapor is released when it condenses and becomes rain. The released heat causes winds, which in turn shape ocean currents.[72] Through the endless cycle of absorbing and releasing heat as it shifts from solid to fluid to vapor and back again, water helps regulate the earth's temperature.

The ocean provides enough atmospheric water vapor to ensure that the greenhouse effect remains steadfast at an average of 60 degrees Fahrenheit on the earth's surface. Warm ocean currents such as the Gulf Stream (great conveyor belt) help make temperatures in the cold zone habitable for humans. Currently, fears concerning the possible impact on the flow of these currents by global warming are on the rise. Some scientists are predicting that if global warming continues to a certain point, it could irretrievably interrupt the flow patterns of ocean currents.[73] The consequence would be a freefall in temperature within former temperate regions, ending at a point far below freezing. With the help of modern technology, humans may yet cope with such radical changes in their environment; but the price will be staggeringly high.

1.5   Sea Routes and Oceans as the Source of Nations' Wealth

In modern times it became clear that sea routes provide nations with a wondrous economic advantage in the form of world-wide commercial

---

[72] This process is generally known as "convection."

[73] Christopher Flavin and Seth Dunn, " Rising Sun, Gathering Winds: Policies to Stabilize the Climate and Strengthen Economies," in *Worldwatch Paper* 138 (Washington, D. C.: Worldwatch Institute, 1997), 10.

trade. The more a nation relies on the ocean as a means of transportation in its trading activities, the greater that nation's opportunity to be successful in its economic effort. World history bears witness to this connection, for maritime nations have consistently garnered the greater economic success and subsequent power. Portugal, Spain, and Great Britain are three shining examples. These three were all once powerful and thriving countries in the past, both in terms of fiscal success and colonial expansion. Their awareness of the vast potential offered by the sea – and their ability to harness it – lead directly to political and economic triumph.[74] Even today, nations remain dependent upon the oceans as the best means for transporting raw materials and manufactured goods. An average of 5 billion tons of raw materials and manufactured goods are being transported by sea route on a daily basis.[75] If all these raw materials and goods were transported over land by train or lorry, how big would the ecological price be, let alone the financial cost of transportation equipment and facilities? Several million lorries would be required for the task, several hundred million tons of fossil fuels would be consumed, and an implausible amount of smoke and greenhouse gases would be released into the atmosphere. The venture would escalate into a runaway ecological disaster. Such would be the negative global ecological consequence if sea routes did not exist or were not used for trade between nations.

The preeminent position that harbor cities serve in their respective nations remains a shining witness to the importance of commercial trade by sea route. The fortune and lives of countless people world-wide are directly dependent upon maritime trade. In the absence of sea routes, land or air transportation costs would outstrip production costs – nations could not afford to remain industrialized, let alone economically successful. Such would be the probable global *economic* consequence of the absence of nautical trade.

Yet another providential function of the sea is its status as the source

---

[74] The colonial possessions of Spain and Great Britain were so extensive and determinative that they have left their marks indelibly on the history of the world.

[75] See Anne Platt McGinn, "Safeguarding the Health of Oceans," 10f.

of livelihood for many people and wealth for the global community. Fishing, offshore oil production, sea weed, coral, pearl, salt production, etc – all are big industries with prominent economic importance. If technological progress continues at its present rate, the oceans of the near future could become the primary source of mineral reserves for the world's population. Another economic boon: sixty million tons of food is retrieved annually from the oceans by fishing.[76] Immense, certainly; but the actual amount of food the oceans *could* produce is several hundred times greater! A total of 2 billion tons of food could be annually extracted from the oceans if companies employed efficient and productive methods. For instance, the technology for extracting protein concentrate is available now. If this technology is widely used in production, then the products could be easily preserved, transported, and distributed. The daily protein requirements for a human being could be produced from fish for less than a penny. Moreover, even more food could be produced if a new and cost-efficient technology is developed for re-integrating the bountiful nutrients of the ocean floor into the food chain. Such a development would result in the rapid increase of fish, yielding an estimated additional 2 billion tons of food.

Another significant economic boon from the sea is its huge capacity for producing electricity. This is accomplished by utilizing the temperature differential of ocean waters. The difference in temperature between the surface layer and deeper regions can be as high as 50 degrees, and this over a vertical distance of as little as 300 feet in some areas.[77] Electrical production works as follows.[78] Propane or a fluid of similar properties is boiled at the temperature of the water on the surface. The gaseous pressure produced by the propane is then harnessed to turn a turbo-generator mounted on a rig to generate electricity. The gases are then cooled again in the deeper layers of ocean water and pumped back to the surface to repeat the cycle. It is crucial that the temperature differential of the given

---

[76] For this and the following, see *Encyclopedia Britannica*, vol. 13, 501.

[77] *Ibid.*, vol. 13, 502.

[78] Power can be also produced from the ocean by harnessing the tides, but this potential is rather minimal compared to that of producing power by using the temperature differential in the oceans.

spot be several tens of degrees Fahrenheit, and the site must also be relatively near an economic center. Most potential sites that could be reasonably utilized are situated in the tropics, where neither the technology necessary for the process nor the markets that would benefit from its implementation are in existence. When the respective tropical countries develop technologically and become affluent economically, however, then much of the electrical power they will need could be generated from the oceans at their doorstep. Production of power in this manner emits no greenhouse gases whatsoever. Furthermore, the practice would lead to competitive pricing: no fuel is necessary for the process, and the plant and other required equipment is significantly more cost-effective than those that use fuel. Some estimate that this process would have a daily yield of about 200 million megawatt hours of electricity,[79] an amount several times that of the daily energy consumption of the United States.[80]

There is still another economic aspect associated with offshore temperature-differential power generation. Electricity produced in this fashion could be used to reduce seawater to liquid hydrogen and oxygen, which could subsequently feed the power plant on the shore. This sequence would no doubt bring about enormous economic benefits, as the energy could be used to disturb and procure the bountiful nutrients on the ocean floor. With the technology for the large-scale production and handling liquid hydrogen and oxygen already at hand, this possibility is no longer a daydream. If the artificial upwelling of natural nutrients could be done on a large scale, it would certainly turn out to be a great help in coping with the malnutrition problem many people in various parts of the world face acutely even today.

The other economic boon the ocean provides is its inexhaustible (and therefore inexpensive) quantity of salt. The usefulness of salt is well-known to all. Salt is used in many ways, most notably is in the food industry. It is essential in food production, preservation, and flavoring. Life would be

---

[79] *Encyclopedia Britannica,* vol. 13, 502.

[80] For purpose of comparison, the daily energy consumption of the United States in 1994 was that of 3.3 million megawatt hours; see *2002 Britannica Book of the Year,* 757.

rather less enjoyable if salt were not available at so cheap a price and in such abundance. Every time a family sits down to eat, their food is flavored with salt. It also offers medical protection from contracting the goiter. Moreover, salt finds wide uses in many other manufacturing industries. It is the main ingredient for chlorine and sodium in chemical industries, and it also serves as a base solution for alkaline and electrolytes. The chemical use of salt to melt dangerous winter street-ice and snow in the West is certainly economical, and it is extremely efficient in reducing winter-related traffic problems. Sea-salt is also the main source for iodine, which is widely used in industries such as photography, medicine, dyes, etc.[81]

New technological breakthroughs have made it possible to convert seawater into potable water at affordable cost. Recently, *Newsweek Magazine* reported that a number of nations have opted to construct several desalination plants: Israel, Singapore, Spain, China, England, the USA, and other oil-rich Arabic countries.[82] No one can gainsay the multiple advantages that desalinized seawater could provide: agriculture, fish breeding ponds, industrial use – all at a much cheaper cost. Coastal areas could become major sources of wealth; for instance, African deserts lying close to the shore could be greened with plants and other horticultural gardening. Such greening would be a formidable weapon in the battle against global warming, and it would also solve many of the social problems faced in drought-ridden areas.

The mineral and energy resources of the ocean are also enormous. With technology capable of drilling oil in the seabed to depths of over 4000 meters, human beings could access most of the resources lying beneath the ocean floor – though it would no doubt be at a higher production cost compared to landlocked drilling. Even at present, much of the world's daily oil requirements come from offshore extraction. Some scientists believe that no less than half of the world's oil reserve could be lying in

---

[81] *The Hutchinson Concise Encyclopedia*, 468.

[82] William Underhill, "Tapping the Seven Seas: New Ways of Removing Salt from Water Are Relieving Shortages," in *Newsweek* March 7 (2005), 44.

[83] This estimation was for the oil reserve in the 1970s; see *Encyclopedia Britannica*, vol. 13, 502.

wait beneath the sea. Further approximation puts the ocean oil reserve at about 2 *trillion* barrels,[83] and *Scientific American* magazine reports that about 25% of the world's oil and gas reserves lies in the Arctic Circle alone. Natural gas hydrates, ice-like crystal solids trapped beneath the permafrost in the arctic, theoretically contain more energy than all conventional reserves of oil, natural gas, and coal combined.[84]

These mineral resources are undoubtedly as remarkable as energy resources. Sea-floor phosphate deposits occur on the coastal shelves of many countries.[85] The phosphate deposit in the shallow waters of Mexico's west coast could contain as much as 20 billion tons of recoverable phosphate rock.[86] An estimated 10^{16} tons of calcareous ooze, formed by deposits of calcareous shells and the skeletons of plankton, cover a wide area of the ocean floor. Some of these deposits lie within a few hundred miles of the coastal shore and have significant commercial potential. In terms of chemical composition, these oozes bear similarity to limestone, and could thus be used in the manufacturing of cement. Another 10^{16} tons of red clay covers about 104 million square kilometers of ocean floor. Aside from its obvious commercial benefits, this clay undoubtedly contains some precious metals; it could also hold substantial amounts of common (but nonetheless important) metals such as alumina, copper, nickel, cobalt, etc.

This magnitude of mineral resources under the sea is mainly encapsulated within manganese nodules. Current estimates yield 1.5 trillion tons of manganese nodules under the Pacific alone. The following chart reveals the metallic composition of Pacific nodules and reckons the number of years these reserves would last as sources for industrial consumption.[87]

---

[84] Rodger Doyle, "Melting at the Top," in *Scientific America*, vol. 292, No. 2 (February 2005), 17.

[85] Phosphate is used as the main ingredient in the manufacturing of artificial fertilizer.

[86] For this and the following, see *Encyclopedia Britannica*, vol. 13, 503.

[87] *Ibid.*, vol. 13, 504.

Mineral	Amount	Reserves at Consumption (billion tons)	Approximate Land Reserves
1. Magnesium	25	600,000	*
2. Aluminum	43	20,000	100
3. Titanium	9.9	2,000,000	*
4. Vanadium	0.8	400,000	*
5. Manganese	358	400,000	100
6. Iron	207	2,000	500
7. Cobalt	5.2	200,000	40
8. Nickel	14.7	150,000	100
9. Copper	7.9	6,000	40
10. Zinc	0.7	1,000	100
11. Gallium	0.015	150,000	-
12. Zirconium	0.93	100,000	100
13. Molybdenum	0.77	30,000	500
14. Silver	0.001	100	100
15. Lead	1.3	1,000	40

Note: The asterisk mark denotes the present reserves are so large as to be essentially unlimited at the rate of present consumption.

Exploiting the enormity of natural resources that lie on and beneath the ocean floor would yield untold wealth through numerous new jobs and commercial end products. It would also make significant diplomatic contributions, for nations would have an unprecedented opportunity to work together in extracting and processing the raw material.

1.6 The Earth as a God-Prepared Dwelling Place

A brief view of the planet earth marks it as unique in the way it is structured and positioned in the universe. As Pascal once described, the world is indeed full of meaning. The atmosphere, the oceans, the molten core in the innermost part of the earth, the existence of the ozone layer, the precise mixture of atmospheric gases – all have profound implications for the continuation and prosperity of life.

Metaphorically, the earth is a well-designed and constructed house. The atmosphere above is a protective shield, much like the roof. It offers protection from the destructive ultraviolet rays from the sun. The magnetosphere guards against the attack of meteorites, just as four solid walls guard against unwanted intruders. This stable atmospheric envelope allows for efficient air travel and radio communication, both vital amenities that make "life at home" so pleasant and comfortable. The vast ocean – our "backyard" – is an inexhaustible source of water. It supplies water with such regularity and certainty that most of the time one fails to notice this particular piece of providence and simply takes it for granted. The wide expanse of land is a garden, providing enough growing space for all the foodstuffs one would ever need. It also affords an abundance of minerals, and its forests play a vital role in the maintenance of life-supporting gaseous elements like CO_2, O_2, N_2, O_3 and water. The atmosphere is "air conditioning" that provides warmth when heat is required and cools down when it gets too hot. Like the loving embrace of a mother's womb, it makes life bountiful and comfortable, supplying the needed air to keep it going and growing. Even the molten core inside the earth provides us with something significant; like a night-light in a hallway, its magnetic field shows sailors the way to navigate safely across wide seas. As discussed above, it also protects the biosphere from the attack of solar storms. The salt content in the seawater carries profound implications ecologically and providentially, for it is an effective natural mechanism in keeping the evaporation rate constant and the ocean currents flowing smoothly. And the oceans are ultimately an immense inventory, a gigantic "pantry" stockpiling "canned goods", natural resources for future use.

Because of the natural protection and care that the planet earth provides, theologians such as Sallie McFague have likened nature in its relation to human beings with the loving bond between mother and child.[88] Metaphorically, the resemblance between a loving human mother and the nurturing power of nature is evident in the manner a mother's womb

---

[88] Cf. Sallie McFague, *Models of God: Theology for an Ecological, Nuclear Age* (London: SCM Press, 1987), 101-123.

protects and nurtures her developing offspring. As discussed above, the atmosphere serves like a mother's womb, providing security to all life on earth. The developing fetus receives all her nutritional needs from her mother, just as human beings receive many of their physical needs from the atmosphere. It offers clean, free, inexhaustible air, nurturing rain, and a congenial environment. Symbolic "Mother Earth" [89] feeds her children with sufficient water, fertile land, vast natural forests, crops, and resources. The question human beings must ask themselves is: do they really recognize this aspect of nature's bountiful providence? If so, they should give thanks to God and honor Creation by entering into a respectful and sympathetic relation with nature, just as they cherish and honor their human mothers. The result will be a true rapprochement between human beings and nature, and environmental injuries will gradually be cured. Needless to say, human beings would receive much in return for this ecological resuscitation.

Humanity dwells in this vast house of nature prepared by God for them, where they can all find safety and enjoy life. Bound to the natural world as it is, humankind shares in its fate. It would not be wrong to say that human beings are all children of nature, living life together under the providential largesse God provides through Creation. They are kinsmen, and their kinship is present in this bond with nature. The ancient stoic philosopher and Roman Emperor Marcus Aurelius once said that "God is the father of all men, and we are all brothers. We should not say 'I am an Athenian' or 'I am a Roman,' but 'I am a citizen of the universe.' If you were a kinsman of Caesar, you would feel safe; how much more should you feel safe in being a kinsman of God?"[90] Marcus Aurelius' thought underscores the crucial need for all human beings to unite as brothers and sisters under the common bond of nature. The world would become a richer, safer, and happier place to live if everyone simply realizes that they are all citizens of natural world. Just as Jesus declared in the Gospel that God lets rain fall on all alike (Matt 5:45), one can note that Creation takes care of all equally. Nature's "rain" falls freely, providing the necessary resources for social and economic progress.

---

[89] *Ibid.*, 97-101.

[90] Bertrand Russell, *History of Western Philosophy* (London: George Allen & Unwin Ltd., 1961), 269f.

This "house" metaphor goes deeper than mere resemblance. Indeed, the Greek word for household, oikos, is the etymological source for the word "ecology". Oikos, if translated technically, applies to the art of keeping household things in order. This domestic clash with chaos logically extends into the natural order and all its supporting systems.[91] The harmonic order of nature must therefore be kept in balance. The question is always: is the balance being maintained, or is the ecological equilibrium under external attack? As is obvious from the discussion above, nature is not immune to external factors, and the natural system has been terribly perturbed by human activity and abuse. The atmospheric regulation of life-supporting gases becomes progressively compromised as more and more greenhouse gases and aerosols are released through the burning of fossil fuels and other emissions.[92] The magnitude of this abusive aggravation is such that nature's huge capacity to adjust to environmental changes has begun showing symptoms of overload since a few decades ago. If nature's mechanisms continue to be overworked, they could conceivably fall to pieces at some point in the future. And if nature collapses, human beings will not survive the ensuing disasters in the wake of its absence.

Nature reacts and changes in proportion to the degree of the burden laid upon it. Because of this ability to adapt, some have suggested that one should regard nature as a single living organism. Of course, this entails a widening or broadening of what one means by "life". It should not be strictly defined as organic entities engaged in the biological process of inhaling and exhaling air. Sensibility, behavioral responsiveness, and the interdependent biological systems that comprise an organism: should these be the determining categories of life, then nature-as-organism cannot be ignored.[93]

---

[91] Henlee H. Barnette, *The Church and the Ecological Crisis* (Grand Rapids: William B. Eerdmans, 1972), 12.

[92] The air in the atmosphere is so badly polluted that many people are suffering from its impact. *Newsweek* magazine reports that as many as 300 million people worldwide are suffering from asthma because of air pollution. See Tara Pepper, "Waiting to Inhale," in *Newsweek* (March 14, 2005), 50.

[93] German physicist Carl Fredrich von Weizsäcker is so impressed by the coordinated networking of nature that he writes an entire book on the topic; for more, see his *Die Einheit der Nature* (Munich: Hanser Verlag, 1971).

British scientist J. E. Lovelock has adopted the concept of Gaia from ancient Greek myth, and he considers life on earth exclusively from this perspective.[94] *Gaia* is the mythological goddess of the earth. Lovelock does not use the term to embrace a universal or cosmological frame of meaning, as it would have enjoyed in the framework of the Greek pantheon. Rather, he employs it in a limited sense – i.e., the planet earth within the solar system. When asked by his friend, Dr. Donald Braben, why he refused to use the term for the universe as a whole, his answer was revealing. Lovelock explained that he reserved *Gaia* for the presence of life: and, as far as we know it, earth is entirely alone in the "supporting life" club.[95] In short, Lovelock uses the "goddess" metaphor to refer to the symbiosis of earth's ecosystem, or to the earth as a living organism. Lovelock further proposes a broader understanding of life beyond the biological, to which he adds the idea of cybernetics.[96] That is to say: life is a self-regulating, coordinating system of communication and control, potentially defined as either the development and function of a living organism or the structure and work of a machine. His point is that the natural system of the earth exhibits a pattern of coordination and self-regulation similar to both machines and organisms.[97] As already indicated, the way the world behaves truly does resemble the way a living organism operates, especially in terms of coordinated interrelation and functional responsiveness to external stimulation. The only recognizable difference is that nature does not breathe like a living organism.

Contrary to the *Gaia* perspective, however, the prevailing model of nature for human beings remains that of a lifeless and exploitable object. This objectification of nature has its roots in ancient Greece, as well, but from the dualist philosophical tradition of viewing worldly things

---

[94] For more, see J. E. Lovelock, *Gaia: A New Look at Life on Earth* (Oxford: Oxford University Press, 1979).

[95] Cf. Hla Aung, *The Doctrine of Creation in the Theology of Barth, Moltmann and Pannenberg* (Regensburg: Roderer Verlag, 1998), 117.

[96] Cf. J. E. Lovelock, *Gaia*, 48-63.

[97] The Gaia concept should not be confused with the deistic mechanical view of the world, which will be considered later. In the deistic mechanistic worldview, the world is simply a lifeless machine.

dichotomously. The dualist notion was furthered by modern philosopher Rene Descartes, who drew a sharp demarcation between mind and body. This has aided, on one level, the emergence of the subject-object distinction in modern scientific approach, as well as modern scientific analysis. On another level, however, it has reduced nature to a mere object whose sole function is to be exploited for the well-being of humankind. Einstein's theory of relativity is pertinent in this regard: philosophically speaking, relativity implies that all things in the world are ontologically related to each other. The existence and continuation of each entity is made possible by its relation to other things in mutually beneficial ways.[98] The philosophical implications of Einstein's theory run contradictory to the modern scientific method and its implied reductionistic outlook. Einstein hints that we should look at things in their holistic structure – their ontological relationship – and not simply as independent entities. The German physicist and philosopher Carl Friedrich von Weizsäcker has also emphasized this holistic approach, adding that the biblical portrait of the world is holistic in essence. Indeed, we see that the biblical depiction of the nature of things and their relation to each other, as well as the Jewish understanding of the human being, is holistic. The biblical model embraces an inseparable unity of mind and body. What logically follows is a complete lack of methodological distinction between subject and object: the two are seen as bound closely together, thereby complementing each other mutually. The biblical model also assumes the relation between human beings and their surrounding environment as a unity of earth, as implied in the Genesis 2 creation of the human being from earth. Seeing the situation through biblical lenses would really help in establishing a true rapprochement between human beings and nature. Rapprochement would lead to a lasting peace, and the wholeness between human beings and nature would no doubt give a boost to the further development of human civilization.

The conceptual implications of biblical holism and Einstein's theory of relativity are entirely discernible in the processes by which worldly

---

[98] See Wolfhart Pannenberg, "The Doctrine of Creation and Modern Science," in *Cosmos as Creation: Theology and Science in Consonance*, ed. Ted Peters (Nashville: Abingdon Press, 1989), 152-137.

things relate to each other. This brief overview of ecological complexity has shown that there exists a mutually beneficial relationship between creatures and their environs. It is past time for human beings to grasp hold of this interdependence. Civilization will go on, even progress more rapidly, if humanity discerns this relationship and acts accordingly, treating the ecosystem with complete respect. Nature will benefit from this considerate conduct, just as all will profit from nature in return. Jürgen Moltmann even goes so far as to imbed the awareness of ecological interdependence within the human genetic code itself: "Through the genetic code human beings are internally linked to their surrounding nature, the whole biosphere of the earth. What we know as the human genetic code is only one variant of the multiplicity of the genetic codes of all other organisms."[99] Figuratively speaking, this notion portrays the world as a kind of commonwealth, binding all life together through one common genetic code. No single organism holds a special position or privilege over the others; rather, all are fundamentally equal, and the well-being of the whole is very much dependent upon the conscientious participation and contribution of all of the parts.[100]

In light of everything discussed above, one may claim freely that human beings and all other creatures have emerged and prospered here on earth because of the well-arranged structure of ecological systems, the superbly balanced order of the natural world. In some respects, the structure of earth's ecology is so well ordered that scientists have come to call it "a fine-tuning of the universe", a concept the second chapter will explore in detail.

---

[99] Jürgen Moltmann, "Die Erde und die Menschen. Zum theologischen Verständnis der Gaia-Hypothese," in *Evangelische Theologie* 53 (1993), 428.

[100] For a theological underpinning of this, see Salai Hla Aung, "Relational Trinity and Its Conceptual Implications for Asian Community," in *Asian Journal of Theology*, vol. 14, No. 1 (April 2000), 82-92; also see the discussion in chapter V.

Chapter 2

Fine-Tuning of the World

On the question of the relationship between science and theology, astrophysicist Robert Jastrow writes:

> For a scientist who has lived by his faith in the power of reason, the story ends like a bad dream. He has scaled the mountains of ignorance; he is about to conquer the highest peak; as he pulls himself over the final rock, he is greeted by a band of theologians who have been sitting there for centuries.[1]

Jastrow's words vividly demonstrate the true character of the relationship between these two disciplines. Though science began with religious tradition as its source of epistemological inspiration,[2] in subsequent centuries it moved further afield from its origins, progressively contradicting religious faith on multiple levels. Relatively recent advancements in scientific thought, however, especially those after the Second World War, have brought it back closer to religious territory. Indeed, many scientists are gradually finding deeper religious implications to their observances. Some have even advocated that scientific theories and discoveries bear witness to the existence and work of a Creator-God. This chapter will undertake to explore these claims and their corresponding theories.

---

[1] Robert Jastrow, *God and the Astronomers* (New York: W. W, Norton, 1978), 116.

[2] For more about religion's conceptual and epistemological contribution toward the rise of modern science, see Ian G. Barbour, *Issues in Science and Religion* (London: SCM, 1966), 44-48.

2.1 Wonderful Coincidences of Physical Conditions and Natural Constants (the Anthropic Principle)

As the scientific quest progressively unravelled the mysteries of nature one by one, scientists impressed by the amazing coincidences in the world's development formulated a theory concerning the purpose of the universe. This theory would eventually come to be known as the anthropic principle.[3] There are a variety of ideas regarding the principle, but the current scientific climate narrows the theory's field into two versions:[4] the Weak Anthropic Principle and the Strong Anthropic Principle.[5] British astronomer and cosmologist John D. Barrow and American physicist Frank Tipler articulate the theory as follows:

Weak Anthropic Principle (WAP):

> The observed values of all physical and cosmological quantities are not equally probable, but they take on values restricted by the requirement that there exist sites where carbon-based life can evolve and by the requirement that the Universe be old enough for it to have already done so.[6]

Strong Anthropic Principle (SAP):[7]

The universe must have those properties which allow life to develop within it at some stage in its history.[8]

---

[3] It was Brandon Carter who first postulated and expounded the anthropic principle under the rubric "Large Number Coincidences and the Anthropic Principle in Cosmology" at a meeting of the International Astronomical Union held in Krakow in 1973 to mark the 500th centenary of Copernicus's birth. See Hugh Montefiore, *The Probability of God*, 30.

[4] For more about the anthropic principle, see John D. Barrow & Frank Tipler, *The Anthropic Cosmological Principle* (Oxford: Clarendon Press, 1986).

[5] In addition to these two versions, Barrow and Tipler add one more principle, i.e., the Final Anthropic Principle (FAP), which reads as follows: "intelligent information-processing must come into existence in the Universe, and, once it comes into existence, it will never die out." See *ibid.*, 23.

[6] *Ibid.*, 16

[7] American physicist John Wheeler gives a second possible interpretation of the SAP, which he terms the "Participatory Anthropic Principle". *Ibid.*, 22.

[8] *Ibid.*, 21

The WAP can be seen as a careful, guarded statement about the material and physical constituents of the cosmos and their corresponding values with respect to the possibility of life. By contrast, the SAP is an overtly imperative declaration concerning the unqualified certainty of life in the universe. Scientists are divided in their attitude towards these two principles. Some renowned scientists like Francis Crick, Nobel Laureate for Biology for his discovery of DNA, and Stephen Hawking, the twentieth century's most distinguished theoretical physicist from Cambridge, are rather hesitant in accepting the SAP conceptually. There are, however, many prominent scientists like British astrophysicist Sir Fred Hoyle and American theoretical physicist John Wheeler who agree with the logical implications of the SAP. Their thought expounds upon the purpose and character of the universe along this line.[9]

Although a rift exists in the scientific community concerning the SAP, findings regarding the development of the universe to date foster a near-universal acceptance of the WAP. Indeed, the fantastic coincidences of physical conditions within this solar system alone lend credence to the theory. The following discussion will offer empirical substantiation.

Observations indicate that the more massive a star is, the faster it consumes its energy and ends its life cycle. By contrast, the less mass a star holds, the slower its energy burns, affording it a longer lifespan. If the star in this solar system, i.e., the sun, were a bit more massive, it would then exhaust its nuclear fuel more rapidly and generate more heat. Even if life could adjust to such a scorching condition, the shortened lifespan of such a massive star would present insurmountable problems for biological development.[10] Such a star would last only about 10 million years; and though this appears quite long by human terms, it is a mere fraction of the time necessary for the initial cooling of the rapidly expanding universe in terms of cosmological evolution.[11] If the sun were a bit less massive, then it would surely last longer; the problem then, however, would be a dearth of the heat required for life to thrive. The sun, by contrast, is exactly the right size: thus, the burning of its nuclear fuel and production

---

[9] For more see M. W. Worthing, *God, Creation, and Contemporary Physics* (Minneapolis: Fortress Press, 1996), 38-66.

[10] F. Crick, *Life Itself*, 97f.

[11] Cf. Hawking, *The Brief History of Time*, 119f.

of energy is precisely suited to the development of life. This solar energy supply is guaranteed for billions of years to come.[12]

Any average 10-year-old knows that the earth orbits around the sun, and that the time needed for one complete revolution is 365 days, i.e., one year. What one usually overlooks is the remarkable speed of the earth on its annual journey and the consequences for life. The earth orbits the sun at the speed of 18.5 miles per second, i.e., 66,600 miles per hour.[13] This velocity produces what is known as centrifugal force, i.e., a force that moves away from the center.[14] Given the staggering speed of earth's orbit, one can imagine just how strong that centrifugal force is. It counterbalances the severe gravitational pull of the sun; without it, the earth would be pulled in rapidly toward the sun, causing a hyper-elevation in temperature. The centrifugal force produced by the earth's orbital speed, however, helps keep the earth's current orbital path stable; and it is the present path which makes earth's atmospheric temperatures the most suitable for life to prosper.[15]

It is also common knowledge that the earth rotates on its axis once every 24 hours. This causes the daily cycle of planetary heating and cooling, further contributing to the vital temperature regulation so crucial for life. The earth's axial tilt of 23.5 degrees to its orbital plane results in considerable annual variation of the sunlight received in middle and high latitudes. It is this angle which makes possible the regular change of the seasons. If the earth's axis were perpendicular to its orbital plane, there would be no

---

[12] Francis Crick, *Life Itself*, 97f.

[13] *McGraw-Hill Encyclopedia of Science & Technology*, vol. 11, 2. Also *Encyclopaedia Britannica*, vol. 6, 59. This speed is almost a hundred times faster than the speed of sound. For comparison: under ordinary conditions the speed of sound is 1,070 feet per second, i.e., about 732 miles per hour. The most advanced and sophisticated modern fighter can fly at Mach 2.5, i.e., two and a half time faster than the speed of sound. We consider the speed of these fighters highly sophisticated, but it is negligible in comparison to the orbital speed of the earth.

[14] For more information about centripetal and centrifugal force, see *Encyclopedia Americana* (Danbury, Conn.: Americana Corporation, 1979), 190.

[15] Cf. Hugh Ross, "Astronomical Evidences for a Personal, Transcendent God," 166f.

seasons,[16] for the sun would remain fixed over the equator.[17] Most parts of the northern and southern hemispheres would receive minimal sunlight, resulting in a deep, year-round temperature drop and making the peripheral regions inhospitable for life. Moreover, how would things look were the earth to rotate on its axis only once a year, like Venus, rather than rotating every 24 hours?[18] The immediate consequence would be enormous changes in weather conditions and patterns. Certain parts of the earth would have continuous sunlight for six months, while other regions would lie in total darkness. Biological metabolism, plant photosynthesis, and the regular cycling of water would be severely distressed. Even if life could persist in such a situation, it would be stunted and significantly less pleasant. Were the earth to rotate too rapidly – like Saturn, which rotates every ten hours – the period of day and night would be too short.[19] In this case too, life in all its forms would be adversely affected because of the shortened period of day and night.

In the scientific journal *Nature*, Jacques Laskar and P. Robutel discuss important astronomical theories about our solar system. They find the inner planets (Mercury, Venus, Earth, and Mars) to be dependent upon the outer planets (Jupiter, Saturn, Uranus, and Neptune) for their orbital stability and regularity. If the outer planets had less regular orbits, then the inner planets' motions would be entirely chaotic, and earth would suffer an orbital change so extreme that its climatic stability would disintegrate. In other words, earth's climate would be entirely unsuitable for life.[20] Laskar and Robutel also assign the moon a critical role for life on earth. Earth's moon is unique in that it is large relative to its planet. As a result, the moon exerts a significant gravitational pull on the earth. Because of this fluctuating force, coastal sea waters are cleansed and their nutrients

---

[16] For pictorial illustration about the inclination of the earth's axis to the orbital plane and change of the seasons, see *Philip's New World Atlas*, ed. Bill Willett (London: Guild Publishing, 1991), 4.

[17] Cf. *The Planet Earth: The World Book Encyclopedia of Science*, 14.

[18] *The Heavens: The World Book Encyclopedia of Science*, vol. 1, 104.

[19] For the rotation period of Saturn, see *Ibid.*, 114.

[20] Jacques Laskar and P. Robutel, "The Chaotic Obliquity of the Planets," in *Nature*, vol. 361 (February 18, 1993), 612.

replenished. The pull also stabilizes the earth's tilt to its orbital plane, which is also a critical factor for avoiding climate extremity.[21] If the moon were not in its present orbital position, the earth would experience two extreme possibilities:

(1) The earth would have had a faster spin rate, leading to greater rotational flattening. This phenomenon would compensate for the lack of lunar torque and reduce the obliquity variation to the present value. In this case, the rotation period rate of the earth would be less than 8 hours (instead of 24 hours)[22]. A totally chaotic situation for life would occur, for in such a short period of day and night the circadian rhythm, the biochemical processes of plants, trees, animals, and human beings, would be severely upset.

(2) The earth's spin rate did not increase to offset the lack of lunar torque but continued to rotate at the present rate. The obliquity of the earth would therefore be chaotic with very large variations, resulting in an increase of more than 50 degrees centigrades in a few million years and even, in the long term, more than 85 degrees.[23] This shift would alter the earth's climate dramatically.[24]

Yet another factor that makes life on earth possible is the extraordinary physical properties of water.[25] Water is one of the few substances that expand when frozen.[26] Most other substances become denser when frozen, and they sink if placed in a container of the same substance in liquid form.

---

[21] For more see J. Laskar, F. Joutel and P. Routel, "Stabilization of the Earth's Obliquity by the Moon," in *Nature*, vol. 361 (February 18, 1993), 615ff.

[22] *Ibid.*, 615.

[23] In its present state the obliquity of the earth is essentially stable, exhibiting only a small variation of plus/minus 1.3 degree around the mean value of 23.3 degree, *ibid.*, 615.

[24] *Ibid.*, 617.

[25] Other remarkable properties of water are its high melting and boiling point and the kind of chemical bond it has. For more information about the unique properties of water and their implications, see J. D. Barrow and F. Tipler, *The Anthropic Cosmological Principle*, 524-541.

[26] Cf. *Ibid.*, 524.

But because water expands when frozen, it displays the unusual characteristic of floating on top of its liquid form. When rivers and lakes freeze in the winter, they freeze from the top down; if ice behaved like other substances, it would sink, and rivers and lakes would freeze from the bottom up.[27] All bodies of water would eventually become solid chunks of ice. The consequences, as one can imagine, would be formidable. All the regions in the current temperate zone would become too cold for life in the winter, because the frozen water in the seas would stop the flow of warm ocean currents from tropical regions. Other unpredictable changes of weather and climate would accompany such an event, presenting serious challenges to the continuation of life.

It is clear that the above coincidences of physical conditions have allowed life to emerge and prosper on this planet. Even more important, however, are the natural constants of the universe which pave the way for the emergence of these physical circumstances. To be sure, more and more universal constants will be revealed as science advances to higher levels of discernment in the future. Some of the important cosmic constants of which we are currently aware are provided by the astrophysicist Hugh Ross in his proof of the "fine-tuning" of the universe:[28]

1.   **Strong nuclear force constant**
   - If larger: no hydrogen; the nuclei essential for life would be unstable

   - If smaller: no elements other than hydrogen

2.   **Weak nuclear force constant**
   - If larger: too much hydrogen converted to helium in the big bang, hence too much heavy element material made by star burning; no expulsion of heavy elements from stars

   - If smaller: too little helium produced from big bang, hence too little heavy element material made by star burning; no expulsion of heavy elements from stars

---

[27] Cf. *Ibid.*, 533.

[28] See Hugh Ross, "Astronomical Evidences for a Personal, Transcendent God," 160-162. For more information about Ross' enumeration of the 57 natural factors in proof of the fine-tuning of the universe, see *Ibid.*, 160-169.

3.   **Gravitational force constant**

   - If larger: stars would be too hot and would burn up quickly and unevenly

   - If smaller: stars would remain so cool that nuclear fusion would never ignite, hence no heavy element production

4.   **Electromagnetic force constants**

   - If larger: insufficient chemical bonding; elements more massive than boron would be too unstable for the fissionprocess

   - If smaller: insufficient chemical bonding

5.   **Ratio of electromagnetic force constant to gravitational force constant**

   - If larger: no stars less than 1.4 solar mass, hence short and uneven stellar burning

   - If smaller: no stars more than 0.8 solar mass, hence no heavy element production

6.   **Expansion rate of the universe**

   - If larger: no galaxy formation

   - If smaller: universe would have collapsed prior to star formation

7.   **Ground state energy level for ^{4}He**

   - If larger: insufficient carbon and oxygen[29]

   - If smaller: insufficient carbon and oxygen

Because of a) the scientific implications of the above constants of the universe and b) the wonderful coincidences of physical conditions in our solar system, the logical cogency and rationality of both WAP and SAP can hardly be denied. Based on the conceptual implications of the above

---

[29] The importance of this ground state energy level of ^{4}He for the formation of Carbon, the most fundamental element for the hydrocarbon-based form of life, is first postulated and expounded by Fred Hoyle, and on account of this he is widely recognized and respected in the scientific community. For more about his explanation, see his *Home is Where the Wind Blows: Chapters from a Cosmologist's Life* (Mill Valley, CA: University Science Books, 1994), 263-267.

discussion, one could persuasively argue that the development our solar system at least, if not the whole universe, appears to have a final goal: the fulfilment of all requirements necessary for the emergence of a final rational observer, namely, the human being. The following discussion will investigate the defensibility of this potentially radical claim.

2.2   Life-Supporting Chemicals in the World

Biologists have learned that all living organisms – higher and lower, vertebrate and invertebrate – exhibit profound chemical similarity in their biological makeup. Indeed, the basic chemical composition of life is so consistent that scientists speak of the uniformity of life in the world when they discuss biochemical formation and functions in general.[30] The sort of life to be found here on earth is chemically composed of hydrocarbon compounds composed of oxygen, hydrogen, nitrogen and carbon. Life as we know it is therefore categorized as strictly hydrocarbon-based. When it comes to human beings, fully 96% of body weight comes from the total mass of the hydrocarbon elements. They are present throughout in multiple forms such as DNA, RNA, proteins, lipids, sugars, etc.[31] The breakdown of this percentage according to element is:

- oxygen (65.0%)

- carbon (18.0%)

- hydrogen (10.0%)

- nitrogen (3.0%)

The remaining 4% of human body weight is composed of what is known as alkaline elements. The exact figures are:

- calcium (2.0%)

- phosphorus (1.1%)

- potassium (0.35%)

---

[30] Cf. Francis Crick, *Life Itself*, 37-48.

[31] For all of these percentage figures, see *The Hutchinson Concise Encyclopedia*, 445.

- sulfur (0.25%)

- sodium (0.15%)

- chlorine (0.15%)

Other elements which play vital roles in biochemical functions and physiological metabolism are found only in negligible amounts and are thus known as trace elements. These include: magnesium, iron, manganese, copper, iodine, cobalt, and zinc.

The main four elements (O, C, H, N) are the primary players in forming life's most basic and vital macromolecules (i.e., long chains of molecule). These chains are the nucleic acids, the proteins, and the polysaccharides.[32] The entire corpus of known life forms fundamentally consists of these three building blocks. Nucleic acids and proteins are the warp and weft of DNA and RNA, and polysaccharides are the sources of energy required by the human body to smoothly carry out both basic biological functions and complex physical activities. The availability of the "main four" and their quantity within earth's atmosphere will comprise the next section of this discussion.

2.3   Proportions of these Chemicals and the Prosperity of Life

To recapitulate: the emergence and continuation of life is directly dependent upon the four most basic elements. The question is, could life have emerged and developed on earth had there been a shortage of any or all of these elements – especially oxygen, which makes up 65% of human body? Researchers theorize that earth was short of oxygen during the primordial period. Accordingly, there were no living organisms of any kind, including surface vegetation. The first organisms that appeared on earth were tiny anaerobic organisms (i.e., organisms which did not need oxygen for life) and sea algae.[33] The anaerobic organisms and algae produced oxygen through the process of photosynthesis, thereby gradually supplying the atmosphere with oxygen, the most fundamental element

---

[32] Francis Crick, *Life Itself*, 39f.

[33] See Richard Monastersky, "The Rise of Life on Earth," in *National Geographic*, vol. 193, No. 3 (March 1998), 58-81.

for life. The emergence of oxygen gave rise in turn to the emergence of ozone. Life thus provided for life: the crucial atmospheric shield, the ozone layer, allowed more advanced life forms to emerge and prosper. The current proportional percentage of atmospheric constituents is as follows:

- Nitrogen, 78.1%

- Oxygen, 20.9%

- Water, 1%

Ozone, methane, nitrous oxide and Carbon dioxide, about 0.1%.[34] Oxygen, the source and spring of organic life, constitutes only 21% of the atmosphere. What would happen if this percentage were slightly larger? Though oxygen is crucial to life processes, any increase of its proportion would be overwhelmingly detrimental. If there were even a 3% increase in oxygen to a level of 24%, destructive fires caused by natural events like lightning would frequently erupt and be almost impossible to control.[35] Objects normally cool and stable would become easily flammable. On the other hand, if there were a lesser percentage of oxygen, the formation of ozone would diminish, and life would again be exposed to deadly solar sun radiation. In short, 21% of oxygen in the atmosphere is exactly the right ratio, which when considered scientifically is (paradoxically) nothing short of miraculous.

Next in line is the element nitrogen, the atmosphere's most abundant component. As somewhat vaguely described above, nitrogen is fundamental in providing nutrients to earth's vegetation. During thunderstorms, millions of lightning bolts around the earth each day combine nitrogen with oxygen. These nitrate compounds that are carried to earth by rain, where they are absorbed by plants as a natural fertilizer.[36] If the nitrogen proportion were larger than 78%, more nitrate compounds would be formed by lightning, thereby increasing the greenhouse gas

---

[34] *Intergovernmental Panel on Climate Change 2001*, 87f. See also Chapter 1 of this book for more detailed information.

[35] Joseph Needham, "The Cosmic Setting of Human Life," in *Cosmos "Life " Religion: Beyond Humanism* (Tenri: Tenri University Press, 1988), 73.

[36] For this and the following information, see Hugh Montefiore, *The Probability of God*, 48.

density in the atmosphere. It would also increase the salinity of seawater, making it inhabitable for the countless organisms of the world's oceans. If the proportion were lesser, enough nitrates for vegetation would not be formed, and plants would be short of this fertilizing nutrient. As discussed previously, another benefit that nitrogen confers to the ecosystem is simply the mass weight or density it adds to the atmosphere. This mass weight provides added atmospheric pressure, a vital factor in the formation and circulation of atmospheric flows. Without the required density, the atmosphere would be virtually worthless, as life-supporting weather systems would be unable to develop.[37]

Two other key atmospheric ingredients are water and carbon dioxide. Together with ozone, H_2O and CO_2 serve as greenhouse gases, providing the earth the warmth it needs to keep its organic life sheltered. H_2O and CO_2 also happen to be the vital factors in photosynthesis. A lesser atmospheric concentration of the two would thus effect a twofold impact: 1) a slowdown in the chemical reaction of plant photosynthesis and 2) a weaker snare of heat, thus leading to cooler weather. If, on the other hand, their atmospheric concentration were greater, then more heat would be trapped in the atmosphere – a problem the earth already faces at present.

What is fascinating in all this is the veritable absence of hydrogen gas in the atmosphere – even though more than 95% of the universe is composed of hydrogen and helium gases![38] Most of the hydrogen with which the scientific community is familiar is not in the form of free hydrogen atoms or molecules; rather, it is a constitutive component of a compound. The simple fact is, if the earth's atmosphere followed the example of the rest of the universe and carried an abundance of hydrogen, it would not be conducive for life. Hydrogen gas is highly reactive at low temperatures. It would thus react with other gases in the atmosphere to form compounds, triggering a chain reaction leading to a shortage of vital life-inducing gases like oxygen and ozone.[39] Thanks to the relative force

---

[37] Cf. *Ibid.*

[38] See *The Heavens: The World Book Encyclopedia of Science*, 50; also *Encyclopedia Britannica*, vol. 6, 60.

[39] *Intergovernmental Panel on Climate Change 2001*, 256.

of earth's gravity, hydrogen gas escapes freely into space, allowing the earth's atmosphere free to support life as only it can.

One cannot fail to note at this juncture just how wondrously earth's atmosphere is arranged. The proportions of its constitutive components are in *exactly* the right ratio to each other in order to *guarantee* life. The extension of the atmosphere, its importance in maintaining a congenial environment for emerging organisms, the precise ratios of its gaseous elements – everything appears purposefully positioned for the emergence and prosperity of life here on earth.

2.4   Natural Order of the World as Fine-Tuning

Consideration of the structure and natural phenomena of the world thus far reveals a well-coordinated networking of the many natural factors necessary for life. A growing number of scientists now take notice of this well-tuned order and believe it to have profound implications. Indeed, some scientists believe they can at some point in the future develop a completely unified scientific theory to explain the universe. In his book *The Universe in a Nutshell*, Stephen Hawking tackles the challenge:

> How will our journey of discovery proceed in the future? Will we succeed in our quest for a complete unified theory that will govern the universe and everything that it contains? In fact, we may have already identified the Theory of Everything (ToE) as M-Theory. This theory doesn't have a single formulation, at least as far as we know. Instead we have discovered a network of apparently different theories that all seem to be approximations to the same underlying fundamental theory in different limits, just as Newton's Theory of Gravity is an approximation to Einstein's General Theory of Relativity in the limit that the gravitational field is weak.[40]

In light of Hawking's musings, the question whether scientists will be able to develop such a unified theory is still open to future discovery and scientific advancement. What one can deduce, however – indeed, as this project has discussed from the beginning – is that there is an observable and calculable fine-tuning, a holistic coordination in the earth's

---

[40] See Stephen Hawking, *The Universe in a Nutshell*, 175; also, *A Brief History of Time*, 125, 155-158.

environmental framework.[41] Natural phenomena in one part of the world are more or less related to those in other parts of the world. Though Einstein's theory of general relativity has helped scientists in relating and calculating natural phenomena, they require further advancement in order to explain these natural mysteries in greater detail.[42]

But despite this lack of knowledge, the "fine-tuning" of nature remains truly wondrous. The term "coincidence" is often adopted to describe and explain such phenomena. Here one can interpret "coincidence" in two ways. On the one hand, it describes the natural occurrence of several events simultaneously, bringing about a unitary effect by accident or chance. This is further designated as "chance or accidental coincidence", as such an event does not occur often. The distinguishing factor here is the rareness of repetition. One encounters this sort of coincidence often in his or her surroundings: for example, a husband and wife each winning the lottery at the same time.

On the other hand, the term "coincidence" can describe the well-tuned networking in nature that achieves a particular equilibrium through various environmental interactions and appears to remain in this state permanently. It could be termed "coincidence of extraordinary kind", because such coincidence is not temporary but endures in its particular form. To interpret this sort of coincidence as "chance or accidental event" would therefore be conceptually irrational; rather, this kind of coincidence is characterized by its mysterious nature and thought-provoking character. Precisely because of this mysterious and challenging character, one can call this sort of coincidence either "the wonder of nature" (in layman's terms) or "the fine-tuning of nature" (in technical jargon). As this sort of fine-tuning becomes increasingly exposed to scientific observation, more and more scientists are interpreting it as "purposeful adjustments of the world."[43] The following are scholarly quotations concerning the fine-tuning of the earth.

Paul Davies, noted author and professor of theoretical physics at the University of Adelaide, writes:

---

[41] For more, see von Weizsäcker, *Die Einheit der Natur*.

[42] Cf. P. C. W. Davies and J. Brown, *Superstrings*, 1-17.

[43] Cf. J. D. Barrow and F. Tipler, *The Anthropic Cosmological Principle*.

Though accepting that the organization of nature can be explained by the laws of physics, together with suitable cosmic initial conditions, some recognize that many of the complex structures and systems in the universe depend for their existence on the particular form of these laws and initial conditions. Furthermore, in some cases the existence of complexity in nature seems to be very finely balanced, so that even small changes in the form of the laws would apparently prevent this complexity from arising. A careful study suggests that the laws of the universe are remarkably felicitous for the emergence of richness and variety. In the case of living organisms, their existence seems to depend on a number of fortuitous coincidences that some scientists and philosophers have hailed as nothing short of astonishing.[44]

He elaborates:

There are several different aspects to this "too-good-to-be-true" claim. The first of these concerns the general orderliness of the universe. There are endless ways in which the universe might have been totally chaotic. It might have had no laws at all, or merely an incoherent jumble of laws that caused matter to behave in disorderly or unstable ways. Alternatively, the universe could have been extremely simple to the point of featureless — for example, devoid of matter, or of motion. One could also imagine a universe in which conditions changed from moment to moment in a complicated or random way, or even in which everything abruptly ceased to exist. There seems to be no logical obstacle to the idea of such unruly universes. But the real universe is not like this. It is highly ordered. There exist well-defined laws of physics and definite cause-effect relationships. There is a dependability in the operation of these laws.[45]

Von Weizsäcker, German leading physicist and philosopher, asserts:

In the inexpressible beauty of the starry sky God was somehow present. At the same time I realized that these stars were gaseous globes consisting of atoms and subject to the laws of physics. The tension between these two truths cannot be without resolution. But how can one solve it? Would it be possible to detect even in the laws of physics a reflection of the beauty of God?[46]

---

[44] Paul Davies, *The Mind of God: Science and the Search for Ultimate Meaning* (London: Simon & Schuster, 1992), 195.

[45] *Ibid.*

[46] Quoted by Hans Schwarz, see his *Creation* (Grand Rapids: William B. Eerdmans Publishing Company, 2002), 128.

And he also points out:

> The world is built according to the creative thoughts of God, this means in a mathematical harmony. Humanity, created in God's image, is able to trace these thoughts. Natural science is divine service.[47]

In his famous *A Brief History of Time,* Hawking deliberates:

> The remarkable fact is that the values of these numbers [i.e., the constants of physics] seem to have been very finely adjusted to make possible the development of life. For example, if the electrical charge of the electron had been only slightly different, stars would have been unable to burn hydrogen and helium, or else they would not have exploded. It seems clear that there are relatively few ranges of values for the numbers [for the constants] that would allow for development of any form of intelligent life. Most sets of values would give rise to universes that, although they might be very beautiful, would contain no one able to wonder at that beauty. One can take this either as evidence of a divine purpose in Creation and the choice of the laws of science, or as support for the strong anthropic principle.[48]

Steven Weinberg, a Nobel laureate in physics, also writes:

> However all these problems may be resolved, and whichever cosmological model proves correct, there is not much of comfort in any of this. It is almost irresistible for humans to believe that we have some special relation to the universe, that human life is not just a more-or-less farcical outcome of a chain of accidents reaching back to the first three minut*es, but that we were somehow built in from the beginning.[49]

In writing a foreword to Barrow' and Tipler's book entitled *The Anthropic Cosmological Principle,* a renowned physicist, John A. Wheeler, declares:

> No! The philosopher of old was right! Meaning is important, is even central. It is not only that man is adapted to the universe. The universe is adapted to man. Imagine a universe in which one or another of the fundamental dimensionless constraints of physics is altered by a few percent one way or the other? Man could never come into being in

---

[47] Quoted by Hans Schwarz, *ibid.*

[48] Hawking, *A Brief History of Time,* 125.

[49] Steven Weinberg, *The First Three Minutes: A Modern View of the Origin of the Universe* (London: Andre Deutsch Limited, 1977), 154.

such universe. That is the central point of the anthropic principle. According to this principle, a life-giving factor lies at the centre of the whole machinery and design of the world.[50]

Hugh Montefiore makes a very apt comment concerning the conceptual implications of "fine-tuning" for the anthropic principle when he contends:

> It seems to me, however, that another explanation becomes steadily more probable. As the number of 'coincidences' lengthens, and as their scope narrows from the universe to the planet, so it seems to me less and less probable that they are purely random. The laws under which they occur cry aloud for explanation. It seems to me more and more probable that these 'coincidences' are intended and contrived (in accordance with the laws of nature) so as to make possible the emergence of man.[51]

Like those noted individuals, many will see things in the same light and draw the same conclusions.[52] What should be noted here is that awareness of such "fine-tuning of the world" is not confined to the modern age. Thinkers of the past have long marvelled at such harmony and beauty in the created order. The pre-Socratic philosophers of ancient Greece, especially, based their philosophical thinking on wondrous natural phenomena.[53] The writer to the Hebrews states (12:1): "So, then, because we have so great a cloud of witnesses surrounding us…"[54] One would do well to consider the great a cloud of evidences, post-modern or otherwise, which attest to the fact that the earth is a God-prepared dwelling place for innumerable forms of life. This body of evidence points, whether directly or indirectly, to the intelligence and wisdom of the Creator. Together with all living creatures, it glorifies the Creator for his loftiness and greatness. The next chapter will try to discover a conceptual link between this empirical character of the world as a fine-tuned arrangement and the intention and purpose of God from a teleological standpoint.

---

[50] J. D. Barrow and F. Tipler, *The Anthropic Cosmological Principle*, vii.

[51] Hugh Montefiore, *The Probability of God*, 58.

[52] For the conceptual implications and significance of the fine-tuning of the universe, see the conclusion section.

[53] See the discussion in Chapter 3.

[54] The scriptural text is taken from the New World Translation of the Holy Scriptures.

Chapter 3

Teleological View and the Structure of the World

Reading a paper to a Japanese audience, Joseph Needham cites a passage of overwhelming import:

A few days ago I read in a book by a Japanese friend, Nakayama Shigeru, the following passage: "The final distinctive characteristic of modern science which I would mention here is a negative one, the absence of the Aristotelian notion of a final cause, the lack of teleology. The artisan's techniques on which Aristotle modelled his theory " the building of a bridge, the making of a desk, etc. " were, from their inception, linked to a specific purpose, but in modern science and its mechanical and mechanistic view of the Nature, purpose has no place. In the nature of things, bodies and particles are regarded as moving about aimlessly, experiments are designed to control these movements for the moment, but in the broader sense one does not know where 'value-free,' 'non-teleological' research is going to go. More generally, the researcher has no idea where the normal science that he practises might be heading. In short, inasmuch as it has a method, but no end-in-view, there is always the possibility that modern science will run away with itself, using its method recklessly to create avalanches of violence."[1]

He goes on to illustrate the possible outcome of such recklessness:

This indeed is the danger which we must ever be on our guard against. Technocracy is only too capable of being evil and brutal, totally

---

[1] Joseph Needham, "The Cosmic Setting of Human Life," 80.

inimical to human life and this is the ever-present danger when technology is not restrained by the values of religion and the other forms of human experience.[2]

The views of Nikayama Shigeru and Joseph Needham strike a cord in their regard for the attitude and intention that drive modern scientific endeavor. The following portions of this project will appraise modern scientific progress and its relation to the traditional teleological view.

3.1 The World of Creatures not as Product of Evolution, but as a Result of God's Creative Work

Though there were thinkers who articulated the idea of evolution prior to his research, it is usually Charles Darwin whose name is connected with the theory.[3] Current convention goes so far as to view the person and the theory as synonymous – i.e., "Darwinism". Darwin's religious persuasion was decisively agnostic. His conceptual position posits a certain intention in the whole of creation, but we cannot hope to fathom what it is or why it exists.[4] Though Darwin spoke to the developmental process of evolution in creation, the way he understood and explained the concept was not that of evolution in the radical sense. That is, he did not build his theory beginning with the idea that life forms originated from matter and always tend to evolve toward a higher form.[5] Rather, through careful observation of the natural order for long periods of time, Darwin discovered significant variations in organisms, even among those of the same species. The mechanism that brought about those variations was, according to him, the process of "natural selection".

Historically, evolutionary thinking was born and prospered in the European cultural milieu. European thought and culture lay firmly

---

[2] *Ibid.*, 80f.

[3] For more, see Ian G. Barbour, *Issues in Science and Religion* (London: SCM Press, 1966), 81-84.

[4] Cf. Joseph Needham, "The Cosmic Setting of Human Life," 69. Darwin himself understood his theory as merely hypothetical; see John Ankerberg & John Weldon, "Appendix: Rational Inquiry & the Force of Scientific Data: Are New Horizons Emerging?", 274.

[5] Cf. Hans Schwarz, *Creation*, 15ff.

entrenched in the legacy of the Enlightenment and its attendant emphasis to humanism and rational scrutiny. This carried over into the economic sphere, where the process of industrialization had already anchored its roots and made marked progress.[6] Human civilization and culture, it was believed, would progress toward a higher and higher level. Future generations would eventually place the whole of nature under their control, directing the course of history according to their will. Such optimism was the cultural aura of the age, a fervent trust in the limitless might of human reason. Later on, this faith in the power of reason was defined according to the rubric of "positivism."[7]

As time progressed, evolutionary thought leaned more and more to the radical. It was "radical" in that its representatives came to promote the notion that all living organisms had originated from matter.[8] The general modern assumptions of life's origins have been greatly influenced by biochemical studies. As mentioned already, the fundamental building blocks of organisms are the amino acids basic to the formation of protein, and the nucleic acids of the genetic code, the warp and weft of life.[9] Everything rests on one question alone: whether amino acids could be formed through natural processes. In an attempt to discover an answer, laboratory experiments mimicked primeval atmospheric conditions. The result was that the natural formation of amino acids is indeed possible. Francis Crick wrote extensively on the process:

> The idea that the early atmosphere was not like the present one but contained much less oxygen appeared to receive dramatic support in 1953 from Stanley Miller, a student of Nobel Laureate Harold Urey, who passed an electrical discharge through a mixture of CH_4, NH_3, H_2 and H_2O contained in a closed system. The system included a flask of water which was boiled to promote circulation of the gases and which served to trap any volatile water-soluble products which

---

[6] See M. C. Lemon, *Philosophy of History* (London: Routledge, 2003), 168-171, and also John McManners, *The Oxford Illustrated History of Christianity* (New York: Oxford University Press, 1990), 657f.

[7] For more about positivism, see Thomas Whittaker, *Comte and Mill* (London: Archibald Constable & Co. Ltd., 1908).

[8] This idea will be what this book terms "Darwinism".

[9] Cf. Francis Crick, *Life Itself*, 37-48.

were formed and protect them from dismemberment by the electric spark. After a week or so the discharge was stopped. The water was found to contain a variety of small organic compounds, including a fair amount of two simple amino acids, glycine and alanine, found in all proteins.[10]

To make sure that such experiments contained no prior amino acids, Crick explained:

> Many similar experiments have since been done, using different mixtures of gases and a variety of sources of energy and experimental conditions, including passing the gases over heated mineral surfaces. The results are too complex to summarize here except for one striking fact. If the mixture of gases contains an appreciable amount of oxygen, then small molecules related to molecules present in living systems are not found. If gaseous oxygen is absent, such small molecules are produced, provided the mixture of gases contains nitrogen and carbon in some form or other. Some gas mixtures produce a bigger variety of amino acids than others, especially if H_2 is not present.[11]

Here arises the question as to what would have happened if the early atmosphere were not that of a *reducing* type but an *oxidizing* type.[12] Crick found his answer in the idea of "Directed Panspermia":[13]

> Another possibility is that the appreciable amount of the small molecules found in space reached the earth's surface by one mechanism or another, perhaps on comets which collided with it, producing local concentrations of suitable chemicals. Even if they only amounted to a small fraction of the earth's surface, there may have been enough of these special places to get things going, assuming that life can start very easily, given the right environment.[14]

---

[10] Francis Crick, *ibid.*, 77.

[11] *Ibid.*, 77f.

[12] Scientific assumption holds that the primeval atmosphere did not contain oxygen. Oxygen was produced and released by early anaerobic organisms and cellular plants, then subsequently collected in the atmosphere. See Richard Monastersky, "The Rise of Life on Earth," 58-81.

[13] "Directed Panspermia" means that the life chemicals were created naturally elsewhere on other planets and carried to earth by fallen meteorites. For more information about Panspermia. see Fred Hoyle and Chandra Wickramasighe, *Evolution from Space* (London: J. M. Dent & Sons, 1993).

[14] Francis Crick, *Life Itself*, 79f.

Other scientists agree with Crick's arguments;[15] for instance, both Ernst Haeckel, Germany's staunchest Darwinist a century ago, and Stephen Hawking, Britain's unparalleled physicist today, describe the origin of life in a similar manner as Crick.[16] In a nutshell, the stages of their postulations often proceed as follows:

1. The primeval atmosphere of the earth contained a sufficient mixture of the gases needed for the production of life's most fundamental chemical compounds.

2. Radiation from the sun or electrical discharges produced by thunderstorms activated those gases in a chemical chain reaction resulting in the formation of amino acids and other chemical compounds.

3. The amino acids combined each other to form a macromolecule, a long chain of molecules called protein.

4. The protein in turn gave rise to the emergence of a tiny organism which did not have a nucleus. This organism used photosynthesis to produce sugar and oxygen.

5. With the production of sugar, the time was ripe for the production of nucleic acids (both RNA and DNA) with the capacity to reproduce themselves and control the developmental progress of life.[17]

6. The natural production of nucleic acids further led to the emergence of simple unicellular organisms.

---

[15] For concise but very instructive information about the views of modern scientists and thinkers on this subject, see Hans Schwarz, *Creation*, 54-65.

[16] For Haeckel's view, see his *The Riddle of the Universe at the Close of the Nineteenth Century*, trans. Joseph McCabe (New York: Harper, 1900), and for Hawking's view, see his *The Universe in a Nutshell*.

[17] Scientific speculation about the origin of life is based not on actual fact but on theoretical assumption. This can be noticed in Hawking's following explanation of the origin of life: "Life seems to have originated in the primordial oceans that covered the earth four billion years ago. How this happened we don't know. It may be that random collisions between atoms built up macromolecules that could reproduce themselves and assemble themselves into more complicated structures. What we do know is that by three and a half billion years ago, the highly complicated DNA molecule had emerged." Hawking, *The Universe in a Nutshell*, 161.

Once unicellular organisms equipped with a genetic code came into being, life had the capacity to evolve further towards higher and higher forms. Eventually a multiplicity of living organisms formed here on earth. This process is held as gospel by evolutionary proponents like A. I. Oparin, Robert Shapiro, Leslie E. Orgel, etc.

Whether the natural formation of RNA and DNA would automatically lead to the emergence of biological life remains questionable. Though both DNA and proteins have been produced artificially in the laboratory, experiments have not as yet yielded a single unicellular living organism – the simplest of all living organisms. Here the opinion of Kazuo Murakami, Professor of Biochemistry and Director of the Gene Experiment Center in Japan, is worth mentioning. Concerning artificial production of DNA, protein, and a living organism, Murakami writes:

> As the research on DNA and proteins, which are the most basic life materials, has advanced, it has at last become possible to produce these simpler forms (in contrast to living things) in a test tube, though it takes tremendous time and effort. Be that as it may, no matter how many DNA and proteins, which are the basic cell materials, are combined, modern science cannot produce even a single cell of bacteria, the most simple cell of all. This is because nothing has yet been known about the fundamental mechanism of how the cell materials produce cells.[18]

In light of the above "origin of life" theory advocated by Crick and other modern Darwinists, though life on earth emerged simply, it remains highly insensitive and resilient to its external environment. Given the right environmental conditions, Crick argues, life appeared to be generated naturally with amazing ease.[19] But does this simple explanation correspond

---

[18] See Kazuo Murakami, "Genetics and Life," in *Cosmos " Life " Religion: Beyond Humanism*, 246. Against the DNA paradigm of the time, Murakami asserts: "Even though DNA is often referred to as the blueprint of life, it is not the blueprint of life itself, but to be more exact, the blueprint of protein, i.e., the material of life," *ibid*. Here one can cite the successful clonings in the recent past as a counter argument. The success story of cloning offers no proof that the artificial production of DNA and protein guarantees the possibility of producing a living cell, but rather that scientists are able to produce an exact copy of a living organism from a living cell taken out of its body.

[19] Cf. Crick, *Life Itself*, 80.

to the actual qualities of life that one observes daily with the naked eye? With some exceptions, life is not as insensitive or resilient as Crick would have it. On the contrary, it is extremely delicate, so sensitive that it requires special care and protection, especially in the early stages of its development. One just needs to turn to the animal kingdom in order to find overwhelming evidence to support this fact.

In the higher realms of the animal kingdom, life reproduces in two different ways.

The first kind is that of internal fertilization in the uterus and subsequent embryonic development. This type of reproduction is characterized by the somewhat lengthy gestation period inside the protective womb of the mother. Biologically speaking, this developmental process is certainly delicate and complicated; and the very fact that the foetus needs a mother's womb to develop indicates the necessity of extraordinary care and protection for healthy life. The nurturing environment of the womb further substantiates the fragility of life. The protective environs of the womb, the model for modern equipment developed for the care of premature infants, reveals precisely how sensitive and fragile life is. If life at such a high evolutionary stage still needs such extraordinary protection and nurturing, then how could life at earlier stages be so resilient as to survive and thrive in the midst of the buffeting and battering of a hostile world?

The other type of reproduction is that of external development in an egg, followed by hatching. In this case, too, is the delicacy of life apparent. The foetus is protected by the shell of the egg, and it can develop only at the proper temperature provided by the incubating mother. The eggs will inevitably decay when not properly incubated. Merely the slightest external hindrance – the wetting of the nest by rainfall, for instance – can upset the process and cause the egg to degrade. So: by no means is life as resilient and potent as one would believe it to be. If life is fragile, and both egg and womb attest to the fact, then the challenge will be to reconsider one's understanding of its origins and progress.

One argument for the "resiliance" camp could be the apparent generation of new organisms from dead and decomposing matter.[20] The

---

[20] Scientists doubt the natural, spontaneous generation of life from dead and decomposing matter; see J. Ankerberg & J. Weldon, "Appendix," 277 and 292.

sort of organism generated in this fashion, however, is quite different from the kind of life discussed above, especially when it comes to biochemistry and physical structure. To say that any man off the street can put together a makeshift tent is not the same as saying that an engineer can build a grand and complex house. Such is the difference between the generation of tiny organisms from dead matter and the gestation of higher organisms with infinitely more complicated structures and organ systems.[21] In the real world, it is complexity and interconnectedness that matter most.[22] The proof lies once again in daily existence: the more complex and interrelated a thing is, the higher and more advanced it is technically and culturally. Hawking is correct when he predicts that biological and electronic life will go on developing in complexity at an ever-increasing rate.[23]

In the transition of life forms from lower to higher, a "higher mechanism" always comes into play. With the help and guidance of this apparatus, a higher type of life emerges as the dominant form. To draw a human analogy, developing a higher quality product requires a more advanced technology. More time for creative thinking is necessary to

---

Their argument is that the small organisms that "arise" from dead or decomposing matter are not generated spontaneously but were dormant in the matter to begin with. It is now a scientifically accepted fact that living organisms have countless smaller organisms residing inside their bodies, and that the "new" organisms are nothing but the emergence of previously existing ones.

[21] Some major differences between unicellular organisms and a higher organisms are: unicellular beings breathe directly through their membranes (i. e., osmosis), while in higher organism breathe through the use of lungs; the nucleus of a unicellular being is covered only by the cell membrane, whereas in higher organisms it is also covered by a second membrane; the reproduction of the unicellular organism is asexual, while in higher organism it is sexual; unicellular organisms have no complex and interrelated internal organs, whereas higher organisms do; unicellular organisms and some lower multicellular organisms do not have vertebrate structure, whereas higher organisms do, etc.

[22] For more see Kurt P. Wise, "The Origin of Life's Major Groups," in *The Creation Hypothesis: Scientific Evidence for an Intelligent Designer*, 228ff.

[23] Hawking, *The Universe in a Nutshell*, 165ff.

fashion and implement the technology to achieve the desired purpose. Thus reasoning, design, and purpose all come into play. The new product is therefore more complex, its parts more interrelated than that of its predecessor.[24] This external guidance in a product's transition is not easily recognizable or observable to the outside inspector. For instance, a kid chatting with his friends by using a Nokia mobile phone would not have the slightest idea about who designed and produced the device.

In evolution-related thought, developmental progress appears to be a chance accident, because it is more or less characterized by the idea of randomness instead of goal- directedness.[25] It looks as though organisms develop without an underlying connection between design/form and end. The structure or form they come to acquire is considered a consequence of adaptations imposed from without by environmental pressure or competition for survival.[26] But this outlook appears to be contradictary to how the world – and everything in it – really is. The shape and appearance of worldly things, the form of their interrelated connection, their place in the structure of the universe: all seem precisely designed to meet the ends for which God intends them. This will become clearer in the following sections.

3.2   Teleological View and Critique[27]

The term "teleology" is derived from the Greek "telos," which means "end" or "purpose". The essence of the teleological view is that there exist certain

---

[24] Some scientists have also noted an apparent presence and guidance of a certain principle in the process of evolution. Cf. Michael Polanyi, Personal Knowledge: *Toward a Post-Critical Philosophy* (London: Routledge & Kegan Paul, 1958); and John Wheeler, "Genesis and Observership," in *Foundational Problems in the Special Sciences*, ed. R. Butts and K. Hintikka (Dordrecht: Reidel, 1977), 29.

[25] Cf. Michael J. Behe, *Darwin's Black Box: The Biochemical Challenge to Evolution* (New York: The Free Press, 1996), 221.

[26] These are simply a reflection of Lamarck's idea of environmental pressure and Darwin's idea of adaptation through natural selection.

[27] For some more information about the critique of the view see the discussion in the later part of this section. For the sake of brevity, the discussion here will be confined to Kant and Darwinism only.

patterns or designs in the created order whose existence corresponds to a specific divinely-intended purpose. Originally, this teleological thinking stemmed from the observed harmony and order in creation.[28] The systematic progression of celestial bodies, the reliable changes of day and night, the steadfastness and regularity in the routine of seasonal turnings: all have helped to form the human worldview, even in ancient times. It is no wonder that many aspects of philosophical thinking in ancient Greece were developed in conjunction with the observance of the natural order. Thus the ancient Stoic thinkers cherished and taught their students the philosophical maxim to "live in harmony with nature" in order to accomplish happiness and success in life.[29] The stoics would certainly never accept simple physical gratification or bodily pleasure as the definition for "living in harmony"; rather, the aphorism prompts one to learn lessons from nature and to pattern one's life after the amazing model of constancy and balance in creation. This ethical awareness of the orderliness and harmony in nature also aroused interest in the observation and study of the natural order, paving the way for the eventual emergence of the natural sciences.[30]

The most easily noticeable influence of this natural orderliness upon the philosophical landscape of ancient Greece can be seen in the system of Plato. According to Plato, all created things receive their respective form because they were created after the model of corresponding ideas in the spiritual realm.[31] What Plato wanted to show is obvious: the orderliness and harmony in creation emerges from God.[32] There was no orderliness,

---

[28] Paul Davies, *The Mind of God*, 194f.

[29] See *Evangelical Dictionary of Theology*, ed. Walter A. Elwell (Grand Rapids: Baker Book House, 1991), 1056; and also Bertrand Russell, *History of Western Philosophy*, 260-276.

[30] Cf. Alfred North Whitehead, *Science and the Modern World: Lowell Lectures, 1925* (New York: Macmillan, 1926).

[31] W. A. Elwell, *Evangelical Dictionary of Theology*, 858ff; also B. Russell, *History of Western Philosophy*, 135-146.

[32] A brief consideration of the historical background of the concept of "nothing" in ancient Greek philosophy will be helpful in grasping Plato's philosophy of Ideas. The Greeks had two terms for the word "nothing." They are *ouk on* and *me on*. *Ouk on* denotes nothing in an absolute sense, i. e., a total negation of everything. *Me on*, on the other hand, denotes that which negates a particular

no harmony, no beauty in the world before God took the action to create physical things according to those spiritual ideas. The world remained in a state of total chaos devoid of beauty, meaning, or purpose. Such harmony of existence emerged in the world only after God's creative activity. It follows that everything exists because it has a specific purpose, envisioned and ordained by God before the time of its creation.

It will be worthwhile to consider the conceptual meaning of "truth" in connection with the Stoic idea of "living in harmony with nature" and the Platonic philosophy of "ideas." In philosophy the term "truth" has several meanings.[33] One meaning carries an existential implication employed in conjunction with a *purpose* or *interest* for which a concept/idea/thing has been formed or developed.[34] In other words, it connotes "to meet or to fulfill the purpose for which something is being in existence." The purpose of a pen, for example, is to be used for making a written record of a sequence of events, a person's life, etc. The pen is designed and produced for this purpose alone. Here one can say that a pen has *truth* if it fulfills the purpose of writing. Viewed in light of this conceptual

---

thing in a relative sense, i.e., the absence of something particular that is required to bring a thing to its full realization. See Salai Hla Aung, *The Doctrine of Creation in the Theology of Barth, Moltmann and Pannenberg: Creation in Theological, Ecological and Philosophical-Scientific Perspective* (Regensburg: Roderer Verlag, 1998), 47. For more information about the concept of nothing, see George S. Hendry, "Nothing," in *Theology Today* 39 (1982), 272-289. Viewed in light of this Greek philosophical background, the picture of the world in the Platonic philosophy of Ideas would appear something like the idea of "nothing" in the relative sense, i.e., *me on*. Matter is already in existence, and also possesses full potentiality to develop into actuality, but has not yet been actualized. It is due to God's creative activities according to the Ideas in the spiritual realm that the potentiality in matter has been actualized to a concrete reality. That implies that before God's creative activities, the world was in a chaotic situation, i.e., without order, form, and shape.

[33] For more see Barry Allen, *Truth in Philosophy* (Cambridge, Mass.: Harvard University Press, 1993).

[34] This is what is known as a pragmatic truth in philosophy. For more see *Cambridge Dictionary of Philosophy*, ed., Robert Audi (Cambridge: Cambridge University Press, 1995), 812.

implication of "truth", both the Stoic "harmony with nature" and Plato's "Ideas" could be taken to imply that one must adjust and live according to the truth embodied in nature. Put the other way round, nature contains a hidden meaning embodied in its present *form* as well as in its *behavior* toward itself and other objects in its surrounding environment. That means there are lessons in the structure and behavior of nature. It is to these disclosed truths that one must turn and adjust one's life, conforming to the dictates of nature's lessons. A person's life is worthwhile and authentic if s/he has successfully embraced these truths in such a fashion, managing to live out his/her existential life in a way that fulfills the purpose of his/her being and ontological responsibilities.

Both the ancient Stoic and Platonic models of Truth find repetition and reflection in contemporary thought, especially in modern Existentialism. The existentialist paradigm of structural design and purpose comes to the fore, giving the ancient models new emphasis and interpretation.[35] The meaning of life and of overarching human existence are reconsidered and reinterpreted in juxtaposition to the existential *Gestalt* and the purpose of individual existence. The existentialist regards the human being as the master and judge for his/her own worth and personality. One may fall from *Essence* to *Existence*, i.e., from authentic existence to inauthentic existence, if one fails to live up to the challenges and responsibilities of his/her being. These guidelines are enclosed as well as disclosed in the *Gestalt* and purpose of his/her existence.[36]

In theological circles the most outstanding instance of the teleological view can be seen in the modern theology of *Orders* in Lutheran theology. Surely it was Luther himself who grasped the significance of the idea of order in nature, giving it new shape and expression. Luther did not embrace the cosmological perspective, as had been the case with the philosophers of ancient Greece; instead, he understood purpose in a soteriological sense. Subsequent traditions would add an *ethical* point of view to the mix.

The theological exposition of the idea of orders in nature was soteriological in Luther's teaching because he saw and interpreted it as

---

[35] Indeed, the German word *"Gestalt"* has a more profound implication and would correspond more closely to the original intention of existentialist thinkers.

[36] For more about this, see Heidegger, *Time and Being*.

part of God's salvivic providence for human beings. Because they had separated themselves from God, human beings remained in need of special protection for survival. Luther saw the existence of family, society, community, and state as springing from orders in nature. The prime purpose of these orders was to preserve humanity from perishing due to the enslaving power of sin. Luther's understanding and teaching of the natural orders is most clearly expressed in his thoughts on the Two Kingdoms.[37] According to Luther, the world is under the rule of God in two ways; viz., under God's left-arm and right-arm. The system of governmental institution is the *left* arm of God, by which God establishes and maintains law and order in the world by means of the temporal sword. The *right* arm of God is the liberating gospel, by which God restores the broken relationship between himself and his creatures and brings them into loving fellowship with each other. Through the heavenly grace communicated through the church, God creates an environment for the peaceful life of humanity.[38]

It is quite intriguing that modern scientists should find new interest in this age-old teleological perspective. Some are of the opinion that a teleological argument for the proof of God's existence is possible by paying attention to the wonderful "coincidences" in the universe discovered through scientific advancement.[39] The following words of physicist Freeman Dyson express just such an argument:

---

[37] Here one notes a slight difference in understanding between the two traditions concerning the meaning and purpose of the orders in nature. The Greeks interpreted the idea of orders cosmologically, thus giving a didactive and scientific significance to ancient philosophical thought. By contrast, Luther approached the concept of "order" purely from a soteriological perspective. It thus carried a providential and preservative significance.

[38] For more information see Craig L. Nessan, "Christian Political Responsibilities: Re-appropriating Luther's Two Kingdoms," in *Glaube und Denken: The Significance of Theology for Society* (Frankfurt am Main: Peter Lang, 2004), 169-178.

[39] For more about the application of the teleological argument by modern scientists, see M. W. Worthing, *God, Creation, and Contemporary Physics*, 38-47.

> There is evidence from particular features of the laws of nature that the universe as a whole is hospitable to the growth of mind. The argument here is merely an extension of the anthropic principle up to a universal scale. Therefore, it is reasonable to believe in the existence of a third level of mind, a mental component of the universe. If we believe in this mental component and call it God, then we can say that we are small pieces of God's mental apparatus.[40]

Although the teleological view has been helpful in providing a proof for divine existence and for developing moral philosophy and natural and social theology, it has not been free of criticism. Immanuel Kant found some weakness in this view, especially when it came to the question of demonstrating the Creator-God. One should note that Kant's critique of teleology had more to do with the conceptual aspect than the methodological inappropriateness.[41] Kant was of the opinion that, though the teleological view could produce a very powerful and convincing proof for divine existence, it failed to demonstrate God as Creator of all things. By pointing to the observable pattern and purpose in creation, a teleological outlook can demonstrate the "footprint" of a kind of cosmic architect.[42] But the possibility of a cosmic Intelligence is as far as it goes: it fails to reveal anything about the intricacy of creation, let alone who this Creator is. As far as Kant is concerned, according to the teleological "proof", the universe could have been formed out of pre-existent matter, similar to what Plato once imagined and taught concerning the world's origins and its Demiurge.[43] According to this model, God used a pre-existent medium to create the world according to the pattern and purpose of his choosing. Under such a framework, Creation would automatically be granted some divine attributes, such as the power to generate itself and exist eternally. Kant identified this as a weak point in the teleological view, and he reminds the reader to be on guard when entertaining its usefulness.

As mentioned above, modern evolutionary thought tends to deny a link between the existence of God and the pattern and purpose found in

---

[40] Cited by M. W. Worthing, *Ibid.*, 40.

[41] For more about Kant's view and critique, see his *The Critique of Judgement*.

[42] See Worthing, *God, Creation, and Contemporary Physic*, 37.

[43] Cf. W. A. Elwell, *Dictionary of Theology*, 306.

creation. The starting point of modern evolutionary theory is that everything evolves through the mechanism of natural selection. The form and character which things come to acquire are the outcome of their adjustment to the changing environment. There seems not to exist any special purpose for organisms to be in a particular form and appearance – except for that it suits them to their respective environment and thus helps them to survive. A newborn giraffe has such a long neck because the environmental situation forced its ancestors to develop this attribute in order to reach the leaves in high tree branches. The driving force of modern evolutionary idea is its unyielding faith in the self-generating and self-preserving power of nature and matter. Modern evolutionary thought began with this conviction and still progresses under its banner.[44] The emergence of life on earth is a manifestation of the generative potency of matter, and upward progress in the constitution of living things is proof of matter's capacity to improve in quality and to cope with changing surroundings.[45]

According to modern evolutionary theory, organisms appear to progress without any special goal, save for existing just as they are. This notion denies the logical implications of the teleological view; thus, modern evolutionists tend not to espouse the idea of design and purpose in nature that their earlier counterparts adopted.[46] This apparent lack of emphasis on design prompted Charles Hodge, a leading 19th century theologian of Princeton Theological Seminary, to carry out a sharp critique against Darwinism. Hodge painted Darwin as illogical in his analysis: "God, says Darwin, created the unintelligent living cell ... after that first step, all else follows by natural laws, without purpose and without design."[47] He then sharpened his criticism by calling attention to the complicated organs of

---

[44] Cf. Ernst Haeckel, *The Riddle of the Universe*.

[45] Cf. Hans Schwarz, *Creation*, 8-12.

[46] For instance, earlier scientists like Kepler, Descartes and Newton were very committed theists and carried out their scientific work with a reference to God as Creator of the world. For more, see Richard S. Westfall, "The Rise of Science and the Decline of Orthodox Christianity: A Study of Kepler, Descartes, and Newton," in *God & Nature*, ed. Lindberg and Numbers, 218-237.

[47] Cited by Hans Schwarz in his *Creation*, 93.

plants and animals: "Why doesn't [Darwin] say, they are the product of the divine intelligence? If God made them, it makes no difference, so far as the question of design is concerned, how He made them: whether at once or by a process of evolution. But instead of referring to the purpose of God, he laboriously endeavors to prove that they may be accounted for without any design or purpose whatever."[48] Whether Hodge's teleological critique of Darwinism speaks to the actual characteristics of things in the world is a question that merits further attention in the next section.

3.3   Design and Purpose in the Structure of the World

Though the modern evolutionary model fails to take into consideration the idea of pattern and purpose, one should note that science as a whole is gradually coming to accept the existence – and importance – of design in Creation. Scientists have noted countless observations concerning the intricate configuration of the cosmos, and there are vast volumes of literature on the subject. Ecology itself, as a science, has emerged from the examination of such pattern and purpose in nature. The modern mind has embraced a surge of new interest in cosmology and an attendant observation of the universe. The enormous body of cosmological literature is tinted throughout with the perceived arrangement of patterns in nature. Like the ancient Greek philosophers, whose interest in teleology was both scientific and cosmological, modern preoccupation with cosmology is, in part, driven by a curiosity surrounding the origin and development of this orchestrated intricacy. Conceptually speaking, one could assert that all scientific theories and laws are simply attempts to describe the uniform patterns of nature in mathematical formula.[49]

This consideration and discussion of cosmological structure has no doubt shed some light on this matter already. Perhaps it has enabled us to grasp something about the idea of pattern and purpose in the structure and behavior of nature. Most of our discussion, however, has been concerned with those features observed in the *external* or *outer* structure of the world. The next section will shift our focus to the *internal* and *inner* structure and life of the world, identifying those patterns which collectively

---

[48] Cited by Hans Schwarz, *Ibid.*

[49] See the discussion in Chapter 4.

connote the purpose behind existence, the reason for being. By doing so, we will concentrate our attention on those features that are observable on the macrolevel (rather than the microlevel) of nature's systems.[50]

3.3.1 Self-Regulation of Nature's Ecosystem

There are some elements of truth in the Deistic belief that, after having created the world, God delegated Creations' further progress to the laws of nature.[51] In light of this Deistic principle, the laws of nature are the product of God's creative acts: they are manifestations of his divine will for the world, embodying a purpose for which they are formed and set in motion. If this formula were correct, the implication would be that human beings could access the very mind of God by studying the laws of nature. They would consequently be able to develop an ethical system based on their observations of the divine mind in nature. It is no wonder that certain academics and theologians have proposed and expounded upon their philosophical and theological systems by drawing on insight found in the natural world.[52] Indeed, the type of conviction propounded by Deism fostered curiosity in the way nature operates.[53] This curiosity in turn gave rise to the emergence and progression of modern science, which now, ironically enough, tends to denounce the very root of its own origin: the idea of God.

If one considers biological life here on earth on the macrolevel, it is clear that life in its highly complicated and integrated form depends on a constant and continuous circulation in the supply chains of food, water,

---

[50] For detailed information about the ecosystem on a microlevel, see Heinrich Walter and Siegmar-W. Breckle, *Ecological Systems of the Geobiosphere*, 4 vols., trans. Sheila Gruber (Stuttgart: Gustav Fischer Verlag, 1984), Yvonne Baskin, *The Work of Nature*.

[51] With respect to Deism, see W. A. Elwell, *Evangelical Dictionary of Theology*, 304f.

[52] See the above discussion about Stoic philosophy. To this can be added one of the two main traditional approaches concerning divine self-revelation in the world, viz., the general revelation of God in nature.

[53] Cf. Alfred North Whitehead, *Science and the Modern World: Lowell Lectures, 1925*.

heat, and air. A distortion in just one of these natural sub-systems could pose serious problems for life. Scientific observation of how the world works reveals the amazing coordinated system and regularity in nature, otherwise known as the planet's ecosystem. It regulates itself in such a way that the constancy and continuation of life systems be maintained and proceed smoothly. But this ecological equilibrium is not inherently permanent, subject as it is to countless external or internal influences. The ecosystem's capacity has a limit, easily exceeded when the balance to its system is broken. This self-regulation of nature's ecosystem is apparent when one examines the food supply chain.

Life would perish rapidly without a viable food supply. The main sources of sustenance for both animals and humans consists of grasses, plants, grains, and fruits. By a process known as photosynthesis, plants harness solar energy to convert water, carbon dioxide, and minerals into carbohydrates. These are subsequently stored as starch in various forms such as granulars, fruits, roots, etc.[54] Oxygen, a gas indispensible for life, is a by-product of photosynthesis, and carbon dioxide, crucial in trapping solar heat in the atmosphere to maintain the biosphere's temperature, is utilized as raw material.[55] The mathematical equation of photosynthesis is as follows:

$$6CO_2 + 6H_2O^t \text{ light} = C_6H_{12}O_6 + 6O_2 + 6H_2O$$

The atmospheric content of oxygen is kept in balance because the oxygen produced by photosynthesis is both consumed by living organisms and employed in the atmosphere's photochemical production of ozone. If photosynthesis did not exist, neither would there be life as we know it, for earth's atmosphere would be completely devoid of oxygen. Furthermore, if the photosynthesis process were to stop today, then most living creatures

---

[54] Starch is a long chain of carbohydrates, also called a polysaccharide.

[55] Plants exhale carbon dioxide in the process of respiration, but there is a net uptake of carbon dioxide by plant photosynthesis. See Heinrich Walter and Siegmar-W. Breckle, *Ecological Systems of the Geobiosphere*, vol. 1, trans. Sheila Gruber (Stuttgart: Gustav Fischer Verlag, 1983), 113ff.

[56] See *Encyclopaedia Britannica*, vol. 14, 366.

would disappear from the earth in a few short years.[56] The same can be said with respect to carbon dioxide:[57] humans produce carbon dioxide through respiration, and the gas is recycled by plants as one of the chief raw materials for photosynthesis. The food the photosynthetic reaction produces becomes the source of energy and proteins for all living things, necessities without which life could not possibly be imagined.[58] The consumption of carbon dioxide by plants in the photosynthesis process is overwhelmingly significant, especially when one considers the implications for climate change. Research suggests that 700 million hectares of new rapid-growth trees are required to remove 5 billion tons of carbon dioxide from the atmosphere annually, an amount equal to that contained in yearly fossil fuel emissions.[59] In short, the self-regulation of earth's ecosystem teaches that what is consumed in one part of the natural order is offset by what is produced in another area.

Nitrogen gas is also crucial to the natural food production process.[60] To review, fully 78% of the atmosphere consists of nitrogen. The transformation of this gas into a functional form for plants is called "nitrogen fixing." This process happens in two distinct ways. One requires thunderstorms to convert atmospheric nitrogen into nitrates, whereupon rainwater washes the nutrients to the soil.[61] The other way occurs through the activities of tiny microorganisms in the soil and water. These fixation processes convert nitrogen into mineral compounds to be used as nutrients by plants. The reverse process, known as "denitrofying", occurs when bacteria convert the nitrates in dead plant matter back into nitrogen gas.[62]

---

[57] An addition to its use by plants, carbon dioxides is also absorbed and contained by the oceans. For more about this, see the discussion in Chapter 1.

[58] See *Encyclopaedia Britannica*, vol. 14, 366.

[59] See Yvonne Baskin, *The Work of Nature*, 198. Seven hundred million hectares of land would be almost the size of Australia.

[60] Note that Nitrogen is one of the main components in protein and DNA.

[61] Nitrogen fixing in this manner is minimal compared to that provided by microorganisms.

[62] For more information, see Eugene P. Odum, *Fundamentals of Ecology* (Philadelphia: W. B. Saunders Company, 1959).

There is thus a natural balance to the atmosphere's nitrogen content.

At every juncture, the ecosystem works wonderously as a whole for the mutual advantage of all of its parts.[63] Plants and trees benefit from absorbing and utilizing carbon dioxide and nitrogen from the atmosphere. Human beings and animals benefit by breathing oxygen released from photosynthesis and by feeding on grass, plants, grains, fruits, roots, etc. Both animals and plants share in the regulation of atmospheric gases, thereby producing enough warmth to live comfortably.

The natural circulation and natural wealth of water is common knowledge; nevertheless, a review of this process reinforces the paradigm of ecological self-regulation. Solar heat trapped in the atmosphere evaporates water in oceans, lakes, and rivers. Water vapor cools, forms clouds, and falls back to earth as rain. The vastness of the seas, the abundance of lakes, large and small; pools, ice-capped mountains, rivers and streams – all ensure enough water for the cycle. This same overabundance is true for the earth's heat supply and its regulation. The sun's energy is inexhaustible, and some of the heat that reaches the earth remains trapped in the atmosphere by greenhouse gases. This stored energy maintains the earth's temperature at the right level for life to thrive. Atmospheric heat is directly proportional to the density of the gas content; i.e., atmospheric gas is regulated at precisely the right mass necessary to trap the right amount of heat. An excess in either direction would yield severe environmental damage.

All of these natural phenomena demonstrate that nature not only contains the necessary elements – namely nitrogen, oxygen, water and carbon dioxide – in the right proportion for food production, but it also employs them in cycles that safeguard and guarantee their future availability. The earth sustains its life through a balanced ecological equilibrium of production and consumption; the current swelling of humanity's population and its addiction to overconsumption, however, will undoubtedly upset this delicate balance. As more and more artificial greenhouse gases such as carbon dioxide, methane, nitrates, CFC compounds, aerosols, etc., are continuously added into the atmosphere in mass quantities annually, the danger for destroying nature's stability

---

[63] Cf. Kurt P. Wise, "The Origin of Life's Major Group," 229.

becomes ever more visible. The crucial element in question is the limit to which nature can endure and resist against these artificial incursions within its system. The observed pattern is unquestionable: most human impact on the natural environment is overwhelmingly negative. The rise of global temperature and the growing propensity of natural catastrophies such as floods, landslides, and storms both point to the reality that nature is suffering under human mismanagement.

Overall, this brief discussion about ecological self-regulation has revealed 1) a kind of structural and functional design in nature and 2) a logical link between this design and a specific end: the emergence, survival and prosperity of life here on earth. One could easily call these factors divine providence at work in the ecosystem as a whole. So, too, could one identify design and purpose in the microcosm of individual organisms. The next section will examine the structure of various life forms for exactly this reason.

3.3.2 *Considering the Structure of Living Things*

Every living species on the planet has a distinct physical form, divided into groups and sub-groups according to physical characteristics. Darwinism adopts this approach with respect to classification within the animal kingdom. Darwinism's one peculiar quality in this respect is its assumption that a species' form is not permanent; rather, it developed as a result of physical adaptation through competition and natural selection. New variants thus emerged, and each family of the animal kingdom consequentially acquired a number of slightly different variants between its members. The process of this adaptation and variation among animals is ever ongoing, for competition and strife are always present in nature. Were this not the case, it would then appear a bit odd, as higher variations within families have not emerged within the last few millennia. There is, however, a current emphasis on Neo-Darwinism. Darwinism and Neo-Darwinism share the same conviction that all living things originated within nature and developed to their current forms naturally. The difference lies in their attitude toward the *means* by which the physical form developed. Instead of the mechanism of natural selection, Neo-

---

[64] In light of modern biological understanding, Darwin's natural selection is less tenable in explaining the physical characteristics and mutations in organisms

Darwinists have formated new theories to explain their views.[64]

One such theory was developed by Lynn Margulis, who received election into the National Academy of Science for her discovery.[65] According to her hypothesis, organisms developed their physical forms not through natural competition and strife, but by contrast through a mechanism of symbiosis and cooperation.[66] Organisms aid one another and join forces to accomplish what they could not accomplish separately. For proof, Margulis offered the example of a symbiotic relationship between two cells of different size, with the smaller cell living inside the bigger one. The smaller cell received nutrients from the larger one and passed back the energy it made. When the larger one reproduced, the smaller one reproduced too, and their descendents continued to live together like their parents, the one inside the other. Over time the smaller one became a mitochondrion inside the host.[67] Laboratory testing discovered that the proteins of the mitochondria resembled those of bacteria rather than of the host cells, thus vindicating Margulis' theory. She and other scientists have since proposed that other cellular compartments are the result of symbiosis.[68] The idea is that living organisms developed their physical forms gradually by adding on new traits through this mechanism of cooperation. Whether this is really the case or not remains an unanswered question. Sometimes scientists are

---

because almost all scientists accept the fact that those physical characteristics are hereditary, and mutations in organism are due to genetic changes. Thus all this comes from within the organism, not from outside.

[65] For more about Margulis see her "Molecular Biological Domains, Symbiosis and Kingdom of Origins," in *Biosystem* 27, 1992, 39-51.

[66] Behe, *Darwin's Black Box*, 188.

[67] A mitochondrion is rod-like or spherical body within a eukaryotic cell. It contains enzymes responsible for energy production. See *The Hutchinson Concise Encyclopedia*, 607.

[68] Behe argues that this proposal is not widely accepted. See *Darwin's Black Box*, 189.

[69] For instance, David Raup, professor of geology at the University of Chicago, argues: "Unfortunately, the origins of most higher categories are shrouded in mystery; commonly new higher categories appear abruptly in the fossil record without evidence of transitional forms." Steven M. Stanley, professor of

tempted to draw very important conclusions from a single example, especially when it comes to the origin of life on earth.[69] For instance, as discussed previously, the fact that amino acids and some chemical compounds can be formed artificially in the laboratory indicates that life can evolve naturally. Conclusions of immense significance are sometimes drawn from simple, even accidental evidence. Things turn out quite differently when it comes to the study of physical changes in organisms of higher complexity. Microbiologist Michael Behe is right when he argues:

> The impotence of Darwinian theory in accounting for the molecular basis of life is evident not only from the analyses in this book, but also from the complete absence in the professional scientific literature of any detailed models by which complex biochemical systems could have been produced. In the face of enormous complexity that modern biochemistry has uncovered in the cell, the scientific community is paralyzed. No one at Harvard University, no one at the National Institutes of Health, no member of the National Academy of Sciences, no Nobel prize winner - no one at all can give a detailed account of

---

paleobiology at Johns Hopkins University, argues that "The known fossil record fails to document a single example of phyletic (gradual) evolution accomplishing a major morphologic transition. Hence offers no evidence that the gradualistic model can be valid." See J. Ankerberg & J. Weldon, "Appendix," 280ff. and 271, 275. One must thank God for providing ingenious scientists whose scientific discoveries and inventions have brought about enormous prosperity, convenience and comfort for life. But at the same time, one must be cautious not to exalt science to the place of God. Behe's view of the relation between the origin of things and science's success in the study of nature is noteworthy. He mentions: "Yet understanding how something works is not the same as understanding how it came to be. For example, the motions of the planets in the solar system can be predicted with tremendous accuracy; however, the origin of the solar system (the question of how the sun, planets, and their moons formed in the first place) is still controversial. Science may eventually solve the riddle. Still, the point remains that understanding the origin of something is different from understanding its day-to-day workings." Behe, *Darwin's Black Box*, 9. Frederick Robert Tennant also argues that the complexity of life is so great that the appearance of life in itself points one beyond the thought that mere chance or blind force alone is at work in the universe, see W. A. Elwell, *Evangelical Dictionary of Theology*, 1077.

70 *Ibid.*, 187.

how the cilium, or vision, or blood clotting, or any complex biochemical process might have developed in a Darwinian fashion.[70]

Another departure by Neo-Darwinism from Darwinian gradualism is the "Complexity Theory" of Stuart Kauffman.[71] The theory states, "Systems with a large number of interacting components spontaneously organize themselves into ordered patterns. Sometimes there are several patterns available to the complex system, and 'perturbations' of the system can cause it to switch from one pattern to the other."[72] The idea is that organisms develop physically through environmental pressure, the changes in their surroundings, or the perturbations inside their own internal biochemical systems. Natural competition through conflict is no longer seen as the main cause or instigator of biological adaptation. Behe's assessment of the complexity theory offers a greater explanation:

> For the sake of argument, however, let us suppose that complexity theory is true " that complex mixtures somehow organized themselves, and that had something to do with the origin of life. Granted its premises, can complexity theory explain the complex biochemical systems we have discussed in this book? I don't believe so. The complex interacting mixture of chemicals it envisions might have occurred before life developed (again, though, there is virtually no evidence to support even this), but it would not have mattered once cellular life began. The essence of cellular life is regulation: the cell controls how much and what kinds of chemicals it makes; when it loses control, it dies. A controlled cellular environment does not permit the serendipitous interaction between chemicals (always unspecified) that Kauffman needs. Because a viable cell keeps its chemicals on a short leash, it would tend to prevent new, complex metabolic pathways from organizing by chance.[73]

All things considered, Neo-Darwinism fails to draw any sort of connection between the teleological idea of *end* or purpose and its relation to an organism's physical form. Physical features are a result of adaptation, and their only end is to survive in a given environment. In the real world, however, one observes a close link between form and purpose, indeed.

---

[71] For more about Kauffman's view, see his *The Origins of Order: Self-Organization and Selection in Evolution* (New York: Oxford University Press, 1993).

[72] Behe, *Darwin's Black Box*, 190.

[73] *Ibid.*, 191f.

Ecologically speaking, the end in this respect tends to have a twofold implication: one for the survival of the organism itself, the other for maintaining the equilibrium of the organism's environment. For instance, most predator species possess longer canine teeth and claws, and they also have stronger muscles and jaws to catch and kill their prey with considerable ease. These features enable the predators to survive. On the other hand, however, the very existence of predator-species puts a check on the unlimited propagation of their prey. The former is meant for the animals themselves, whereas the latter strictly serves the environment. Similar examples can be found with birds. Birds are equipped with wings for flying high in the sky, and in this way they can easily escape falling prey to their enemies on land. This end, or *telos*, is for their survival. On the other hand, birds catch and destroy many harmful insects in the air, and they also pollinate plants far and wide. This function is clearly the ecological end of wings.

In light of this twofold implication of purpose, one can infer that the physical adaptation of organisms goes far beyond its immediate need for survival in the miniature realm of its habitat. This runs contray to the idea that living things actually develop and improve their physical structure through natural competition or symbiosis and cooperation. If organisms are indeed in their present physical forms because they are *intended* to be, then their existence and their relation to nature need to be approached teleologically. This apparent link between form and purpose suggests the existence of an outsider in the game, a designer who sees and arranges things holistically. The physical features of organisms, the complexity of biochemical systems and their relation to the surrounding ecosystem: all add credence to the possibility that such an outsider exists.

3.4 Further Consideration of the Conceptual Implications of the Teleological View

The above discussion demonstrates the teleological view to be helpful in showing the hidden meaning inclosed in the way creatures appear and disclosed in the way they behave and relate with themselves and other things in their surroundings. The view draws its strength by forming a logical link between the noticeable features observed in nature and their apparently related purpose. It therefore appeals to the human condition, for human beings are well acquainted with such analogies existentially.

Kant himself recognized the strength and rationality of the teleological argument; indeed, the position possesses such power because it is in line with the common experience and sense of people. Even in ancient times, cultures had developed the view by drawing insight from the beauty and harmony they observed in the world. It is small wonder that Thomas Aquinas based his fifth proof for the existence of a Supreme Being entirely on teleology. In later centuries, Anglican theologian William Paley and Princeton theologian Charles Hodge employed the teleological argument in an attempt to prove the intelligibility of religious faith.

The criticism typically flung at teleology is that the existence of creaturely imperfection and its associated evils do not square with the idea of perfection, beauty and harmony so central to the argument. Why is there such imperfection and evil in the world if the world and all things in it are so "perfectly" designed by a Supreme Being? Indeed, there is much imperfection and evil in the world, but those imperfections are the exception to the rule. They exist in the ubiquitoius shadow of perfection, in the beauty and harmony throughout the worldly order. Pauline theology and Leibniz's philosophy both offer testimony to this "minority" of imperfection.

In Pauline theology evil is the result of the law. The knowledge of the law enables human beings to distinguish the good and the bad, and in this knowledge the true character and meaning of evil is grasped. But the law itself is not evil in Paul's view: "What, then, shall we say? Is the law sin? Never may that become so! Really I would not have come to know sin if it had not been for the law; and, for example, I would not have known covetousness if the law had not said: 'You must not covet'" (Rom. 7:7). According to the logical implication of Paul's understanding, the law helps one to know what evil is and accordingly enables us to live life meaningfully.[74] Put the other way round, the existence of evil gives substance to the law, for the law's teachings about evil gain moral urgency, potency and authority precisely because evil exists. That means that the

---

[74] If literally interpreted, the Pauline argument could mean quite the opposite. But the point of Paul's argument in this text is that it is not the law but sin that has capitalized on the law and induced humans to commit the wrong, the ugly, and the evil, and that these are not what the law is intended to effect originally.

power of the law would become void in evil's absence. Through its knowledge and teachings, the law is a moral corrective for human beings. It thereby achieves beauty and harmony in the social life of community, establishing and mediating justice and order.[75]

Leibniz also noticed the existence of evil, but this never stopped him from adhering to his famous dictum: "the world as the best of all possible worlds." Leibniz observed well the existence of both good and the evil in the world, and he saw the extent to which physical good outstripped physical evil. He also understood the existence of evil in the world as a means to enhance the good: "There is, moreover, more physical good than physical evil in the world. Further, physical sufferings are 'results of moral evil.' They serve many useful purposes; for they act as a penalty for sin and as a means of perfecting the good."[76]

Both Paul and Leibniz suggest that the existence of worldly imperfection, evil, and suffering do not grant one the warrant to deny outright the validity and usefulness of the teleological view.

The teleological argument can provide a wider base and a more profound insight into the hidden truth of life. It will offer a more intelligent interpretation of the Christian faith, especially if the term "design" is defined in a broad sense and embraces coordinated functional systems as well as the complex biochemical structure of living organisms. If the term "design" is taken to imply "the purposeful arrangement of parts," as Behe suggests, then it will surely grant a broader perspective of the love and providence of God in nature.[77] Tillich's view that "divine transcendence

---

[75] This should be viewed as the importance of the law with regard to the question of theodicy, and this might be what Paul had in mind when he refers to the law. The impotence of law in reconciling people back to God is apparent in Paul's argument, but this belongs to the question of soteriology. For more about the implication and meaning of law with regard to the question of theodicy and soteriology in Paul's view, see C. K. Barrett, *Paul: An Introduction to His Thought* (London: Geoffrey Chapman, 1994), 74-87.

[76] Frederick Copleston, *A History of Philosophy*, vol. 9 (London: Burns & Oathes, 1965), 328.

[77] Cf. *Ibid.*, 193.

could not be found in the superficial flux of worldly phenomena, but is to be found deep down in the inner structure and nature of things" will receive greater appreciation as more and more about the functional and structural design of biochemical life is exposed.[78]

The overall structure of the earth lends strong evidence and support to the implication that there exists an intelligent design in the world that carries with it a greater and deeper purpose. As with the anthropic principle, one can argue that the earth has this design because it is intended to meet the needs and requirements of the kind of biological life that emerged on its surface. The relation between design and purpose is ultimately unquestionable, and one can grasp the meaning of life more profoundly if one approaches worldly reality from a teleological standpoint.[79] The important thing for all human beings in this respect is that the relationship between design and purpose not be hampered through reckless and inconsiderate activities. Rather, its should be kept healthy

---

[78] Paley's *Natural Theology*, Hodge's *What is Darwinism?* and *Systematic Theology*, Tennant's *Philosophical Theology*, Behe's *Darwin's Black Box*, Ross' *The Fingerprint of God* and *The Creator and the Cosmos*, and P. C. W. Davies' *The Mind of God: Science and the Search for Ultimate Meaning*, Gerald Schroeder's *The Hidden Face of God: How Science Reveals the Ultimate Truth* all are good examples in this respect.

[79] For more, see Stephen C. Meyer, "The Methodological Equivalence of Design & Descent: Can There Be a Scientific 'Theory of Creation'?" in *The Creation Hypothesis*, 67-112. Also William A. Dembski, "On the Very Possibility of Intelligent Design," in *The Creation Hypothesis*, 113-138.

and strong through conscientious participation in the ecological community.

Chapter 4

Chaos Theory and the World

Regarding the far-reaching implications of Chaos Theory for science in the postmodern era, James Gleick writes:

Chaos breaks across the lines that separate scientific disciplines. Because it is a science of the global nature of system, it has brought together thinkers from fields that had been widely separated. "Fifteen years ago, science was heading for a crisis of increasing specialization," a Navy official in charge of scientific financing remarked to an audience of mathematicians, biologists, physicists, and medical doctors. "Democratically, that specialization has reversed because of chaos." Chaos poses problems that defy accepted ways of working in science. It makes strong claims about the universal behavior of complexity. The first chaos theorists, the scientists who set the discipline in motion, shared certain sensibilities. They had an eye for pattern, especially pattern that appeared on different scales at the same time. They had a taste for randomness and complexity, for jagged edges and sudden leaps. Today believers in chaos " they sometimes call themselves believers, or converts, or evangelists " speculate about determinism and free will, about evolution, about the nature of conscious intelligence. They feel that they are turning back a trend in science toward reductionism, the analysis of systems in terms of their constituent parts: quarks, chromosomes, or neurons. They believe that they are looking for the whole.[1]

---

[1] James Gleick, *Chaos: Making a New Science* (London: Sphere Books, 1987), 5.

On the surface, Chaos Theory appears rather odd; to the surprise of many, however, scientists have found it to hold marvelous phenomena with profound conceptual implications. As Gleick aptly asserts in the above quotation, Chaos Theory has posed new challenges by demanding that the current method of understanding and interpreting Science be reevaluated. The following sections describe these new developments exposed by Chaos Theory.

4.1   Origin of the Theory

There were many new developments in the various scientific fields of the 20th century. The formulation of Chaos Theory would emerge at the top of this list, along with two others: relativity theory and quantum theory.[2] Generally speaking, people have observed chaotic phenomena within natural systems for quite a long time. There is a natural turbulence apparent within specific geographical areas that is indicative of the wider chaotic character of global systems as a whole. For instance, the unexpected occurrence of a local thunderstorm represents the kind of natural turbulence which people the world over have often experienced since time immemorial. This sort of turmoil in nature exerts profound psychological influence on human life and thought, leading even to the worship of the natural order. One should not take Chaos Theory to be synonymous with such natural chaotic phenomena, however, but as a specific scientific formulation developed in the second half of the 20th century.

Modern Chaos Theory emerged in the laboratory of an M.I.T. meteorologist, Edward N. Lorenz. In 1961, when Lorenz was running a lengthy computer calculation about weather patterns, he noticed an amazing new factor in the process. At some point he was forced to pause in his computer calculations, so he saved some of his immediate results to avoid starting from scratch all over again. Continuing the program with his saved data after the break, Lorenz was startled to find that his final results were quite different from those he had gotten earlier when running the same calculations without interruption.[3]

---

[2] Cf. *ibid.*, 6.

[3] George Ochoa and Melinda Corey, ed., *The Wilson Chronology of Science and Technology* (New York: The H. W. Wilson Company, 1997), 290.

Searching for the source of the inconsistency, Lorenz found that the computer had rounded off the figures slightly differently when saving them than when running them continuously. Although this discrepancy affected only the eighth decimal place in the original numbers, it was enough to cause enormous differentiation in the final analysis. Lorenz thus discovered that weather systems are highly sensitive to initial conditions: they are, in short, chaotic.[4] Here it must be noted that the meaning of the term "chaos" or "chaotic," according to Lorenz's understanding, is not understood in an absolute sense, but rather in a relative sense. In an absolute sense, "chaos" means that a system is in a state of total disarray and disorder, very much like the biblical picture of the world before God's creative work. A relative sense of "chaos", by contrast, portrays a system as a complex, complicated, and unpredictable state consisting of countless factors and figures that are not constant but changing all the time.[5]

Lorenz's findings of weather systems on the computer correspond to the actual character of weather in nature, for natural weather systems consist of many factors, figures, and conditions which are very much susceptible to unpredictable changes. Together as a whole, these factors make up one complex chaotic system. This means that one cannot possibly predict exactly what will happen on a given Saturday in one's home town in three weeks' time, because many unpredictable things will occur in the interim and introduce confusion and disorder into the process of calculation. Of special interest to Lorenz's discovery is the weather's special sensitivity to extremely minimal changes, even though common sense would categorize them as negligible, even inconsequential. The Chaos Factor thus paints the world and all its natural sub-systems as

---

[4] *Ibid.*

[5] Cf. William L. Ditto and Louis M. Pecora, "Mastering Chaos," in *Scientific American,* vol. 269, No. 2 (August 1993), 62-65. For more about Lorenz's view of chaos, see Edward N. Lorenz, "Deterministic Nonperiodic Flow," in *Journal of the Atmospheric Sciences,* vol. 20 (March 1963), 130f. Literally interpreted, the term would have the connotation of an absolute sense. The relative sense of the term is a technical connotation and thus closer to what Chaos Theory means scientifically.

[6] For instance, scientists realize that there still exist many problems, even when it comes to calculating climate change, because of the lack of detailed information. See *Intergovernmental Panel on Climate Change 2001,* 59ff.

overwhelmingly intricate, complicated, and unpredictable. Understanding and calculating the world's systems to this degree of minute detail therefore becomes a remarkably difficult task.[6]

Together with quantum theory, Chaos Theory could be revolutionary, especially when compared with the mechanistic worldview of the medieval and early modern periods. The mechanistic model of the world is that of a big machine, perfectly and systematically constructed, fixed in the ironclad laws of nature with amazing precision and accuracy.[7] Scientists in those eras assumed that if one were to know all the fundamental physical facts of the universe at a given point in time, then one could accurately predict how those facts would affect a later point in time. In other words, they believed in the possibility that one could accurately predict the future. The world and everything in it was seen as scientifically countable, calculable, and predictable, since it was governed by a fixed set of natural laws. The natural order of the universe thus appeared to be an absolutely closed system.[8] As far as the maintenance and smooth functioning of the world was concerned, no sort of external intervention was required. A divine "Outsider" was regarded as superfluous and therefore disqualified from the natural order. The world-machine was autonomous, entirely self-reliant and self-regulating.[9]

This mechanistic sentiment is represented succinctly by Pierre Simon de Laplace (1749-1827), a French astronomer and mathematician. Napoleon Bonaparte reputedly once asked Laplace to explain the cause and nature of worldly phenomena. Much to Napoleon's surprise, Laplace offered that such phenomena operated solely according to fixed natural laws. Napoleon then asked Laplace where God would belong in such a system. The astronomer's answer was entirely predictable: the hypothesis of God is completely unnecessary to the mechanistic paradigm.[10] This superfluity

---

[7] Cf. Ian Stewart, *Does God Play Dice?*, 1.

[8] Cf. M. W. Worthing, *God, Creation, and Contemporary Physics*, 162ff.

[9] Cf. Ian G. Barbour, *Issues in Science and Religion*, 35f.

[10] Cf. Roger Hahn, "Laplace and the Mechanistic Worldview," in *God & Nature*, ed. Lindberg and Numbers, 256.

of God is entirely in line with the thought of Auguste Comte (1798-1857). His philosophy of positivism is simply the logical culmination of mechanistic sentiment: science is nothing more than the latest development of human civilization in the history of humankind hitherto.

According to positivism, there are three stages in the developmental history of knowledge. The first and earliest stage was the theological, in which humankind explained natural phenomena by appealing to the existence of higher spiritual beings, i.e., gods or God. The next stage was the metaphysical, in which these beings become depersonalized forces or essences. The final (and current) stage is the positive, in which phenomena are explained according to scientific theory and description.[11] Given the progress of scientific research and the prevailing academic in Comte's time, it is no surprise that positivists denied the relevance of metaphysics to their philosophy. The idea that everything should be studied and judged within the bounds of science lies at the very core of their thought-world. Positivism's logic simply asserts that the way science describes the world is completely accurate, accountable, and trustworthy. For science is nothing more than the product of observation and experiment concerning the existence and operation of the immutable and lasting laws of nature, the forces that join all parts of the world-machine together.

Unsurprisingly, the mechanistic worldview and its concomitant positivistic philosophy spawned a new theological outlook in religious circles. As hinted above, this movement is known as "Deism," a direct derivation from the Latin word for God ("deus"). Deism served as counterbalance as well as complement to the mechanistic worldview and the positivistic philosophy. On the one hand, it is a corrective in that it took the mechanistic structure of the world to be a result of purposeful divine thought and action.[12] Thus one could not fully understand the world without reference to the divine purpose and intention enclosed within nature. God, according to Deism, is the prime cause of the world's mechanistic structure. Metaphysics is therefore important in understanding the way of things because the purpose of existence is rooted not within

---

[11] Cf. W. A. Elwell, *Evangelical Dictionary of Theology*, 864.

[12] Cf. *ibid.*, 304.

[13] Cf. P. Davies, *The Mind of God*, 31.

nature (physic) but beyond it (meta-physic).[13] For the Deists, Metaphysics is crucial to understanding the purpose of existence in its totality.

On the other hand, however, Deism complements the mechanistic worldview because it constructs its theology according to the same main principle, i.e. determinism. According to this principle, everything is predetermined through the workings of natural laws. Nature is the complete revelation of divine wisdom and will. This revelation is so fundamental, direct, and sufficient, that no further revelation required for understanding God.[14] The deists therefore deny any validity to the biblical doctrines of divine incarnation, intervention, special providence for salvation, etc.[15] One can learn divine will and purpose entirely in nature, and salvation is attainable by conforming to the ethical commands and teachings of natural truths embedded and revealed in the natural world.

Deistic materialists were far from exercising a cosmological monopoly. Other thinkers of the time, like Decartes, Newton, Kepler, and Leibniz, took the existence and operation of the laws of nature to be divine intervention. This providential perspective actually encouraged study of the world's relationship to underlying laws[16]; in other words, trust in the dependability of divine providence laid a necessary foundation for scientists like Newton to observe and study nature and its laws. Even modern thinkers such as Einstein took the implication and significance of natural laws seriously. Einstein will always be well remembered not only for his genius in formulating the theory of relativity but also for his deep suspicion concerning the validity of quantum theory.[17] His unwavering faith in the working of fixed natural laws is evident in the following line from a letter to his friend, Max Born: "You believe in a God who plays dice, and I in complete law and order."[18] Given all of these factors, one can truthfully claim that the mechanistic worldview, with its staunch

---

[14] Cf. W. A. Elwell, *Evangelical Dictionary of Theology*, 304f.

[15] *Ibid.*

[16] Cf. J. D. Barrow, *Theory of Everything*, 12f.

[17] See Hawking, *A Brief History of Time*, 56.

[18] Ian Stewart, *Does God Play Dice?*, 1. Max Born is a Nobel laureate for physics in 1954 for his work on quantum theory.

emphasis on the immutability of natural laws, gave impetus to the further development of modern science.

As each successive modern scientific discovery uncovered more and more of nature's secrets, were the mechanistic worldview gradually lost its influential power. Modern science has been very much successful in studying and demonstrating the structure and nature of things even at the sub-atomic level. Such findings reveal that the structure and behavior of physical reality defies the prior assumptions of medieval and early modern thought. New laws of nature are being discovered one after another, and some of them contradict completely their earlier counterparts. With these contradictions come new conceptions regarding the structure and behavior of the world. The universe is no longer seen as a closed system, but as an open one. Likewise, the machine-image of reality has been replaced by the image of a living world-organism with generative creativity, potentiality, and adaptability as its new symbols. No longer is the world a static, designed machine with indestructible and irreplaceable nuts and bolts at every joint. It is rather like a life-form, destined to grow up, age, and finally expire.[19]

Stephen Hawking succinctly describes the relation between the newly formulated theory of postmodern science and the demise of the mechanistic determinism as follows:

> The uncertainty principle signaled an end to Laplace's dream of a theory of science, a model of the universe that would be completely deterministic: one certainly cannot predict future events exactly if one cannot even measure the present state of the universe precisely![20]

Indeed, according to the picture of the world illustrated by postmodern science, the universe can be considered a chaotic system on both the microscopic and macroscopic levels. Microscopic findings demonstrate that the world is characterized by a complicated and unpredictable nature.[21]

---

[19] For instance, the formulation of the second law of thermodynamics clearly demonstrates that the world system cannot go on forever because the availability of energy is limited. See M. W. Worthing, *God, Creation, and Contemporary Physics,* 79f.

[20] S. Hawking, *A Brief History of Time,* 55.

[21] For more, see the discussion in the following section.

Likewise, things turn out to be quite convoluted and irreconcilable with each other on the cosmic level. Once, scientists like Einstein hoped that they could formulate a unified theory of relativity that could explain everything in the cosmos. So far, it hasn't worked. The unpredictability of the nature and behavior of subatomic particles staunchly defies any effort to explain everything in the universe with a single unified theory.

> Things become even mind-boggling when one tries to explain the development of the universe in every detail. Hawking vividly notes such difficulty in the following statement:

> In previous chapters I have described general relativity, the partial theory of gravity, and the partial theories that govern the weak, the strong, and the electromagnetic forces. The last three may be combined in so-called grand unified theories, or GUTs, which are not very satisfactory because they do not include gravity and because they contain a number of quantities, like the relative masses of different particles, that cannot be predicted from the theory but have to be chosen to fit the observations. The main difficulty in finding a theory that unifies gravity with the other forces is that general relativity is a "classical" theory; that is, it does not incorporate the uncertainty principle of quantum mechanics. On the other hand, the other partial theories depend on quantum mechanics in an essential way. A necessary first step, therefore, is to combine general relativity with the uncertainty principle... The trouble is, the uncertainty principle means that even "empty" space is filled with pairs of virtual particles and antiparticles. These pairs would have an infinite amount of energy and, therefore, by Einstein's famous equation $E = mc^2$, they would have an infinite amount of mass. Their gravitational attraction would thus curve the universe to infinitely small size.[22]

Hawking's view demonstrates that it is tremendously difficult to give constructive speculation with respect to the present state of the world, let alone with respect to the origin and destination of the cosmos. An immense amount of unpredictability enters the process as one attempts to plot the developmental course of the universe. The structure and nature of the universe as a whole thus exhibits an unquestionable chaotic quality.

The macroscopic level, too, illuminates the world's systems as

---

[22] S. Hawking, *A Brief History of Time*, 156f.

[23] Cf. Yvonne Baskin, *The Working of Nature*, 223.

uncompromisingly chaotic. The two most easily observable natural systems of the world, i.e., the ecosystem and the weather system, are wonderful examples thereof. The ecological arena is as vast, intricate, and mysterious as the universe itself. Detailed scientific study of local ecosystems in many corners of the globe is yet to be carried out.[23] Comprehensive and exhaustive information about the ecosystem on a global level remains a distant reality. Even the limited studies already accomplished prove the ecosystem to be more marvelous and mystifying than anyone ever thought possible.[24] A range of conditions and circumstances are involved in the ecology of a given climate. What makes studying a local ecosystem so confounding is the constant moving, changing, birth, and dying of its various populations. The interaction between these factors and the positive and negative influences they exert within the system as a whole is difficult to plot; a precise prediction concerning the area's ecological future is thus virtually impossible. In any case, that the ecosystem of any area is highly susceptible to changes within the environment is certain, and its future is very much dependent upon a well-maintained balance of all the factors involved. In other words, its future is open: it remains uncertain and unpredictable.

The same can be said about weather systems. As with the ecosystem, the world's weather systems consist of numerous factors, conditions, and circumstances. For instance, in order to calculate the weather for any given area, one needs to know the air pressure, wind direction, state of cloud formation, land temperature of the last few days, rate of evaporation, etc. All of these factors, of course, can change within the span of a few hours, introducing acute confusion into the calculation. When computing the weather on a global scale, the number of factors and changes to consider increases exponentially. Again, what Lorenz was calculating on his computer was only the weather for a localized area. Hence he had to deal with fewer numbers, figures, and factors, allowing for fewer equations.[25] Global weather prediction would involve the input of countless more figures and accordingly more equations. The global weather system is a complicated and confusing network, the end result of which remains

---

²⁴ Cf. *Ibid.*, 21f.

²⁵ Cf. E. N. Lorenz, "Deterministic Nonperiodic Flow," 131-140.

entirely dependent upon the co-creative and correlate relations of numerous factors.

Such a strong connection among the relevant factors of a finely functioning system is yet another indicator of chaos. Once again: Chaos Theory does not signify a system in total disarray and disorder, but one in which countless circumstances and changes come together to make the system more complex and confusing. The idea that there can be harmony, beauty, and progress in a system when all the involved factors are connected through mutually beneficial, balanced participation.[26] What follows from this logically is that the balance hangs on the actual implementation of the semantic content of a series of words: co-creative, correlative, symmetrical, mutually beneficial. But how is such a connection between such an exorbitant number of factors accomplished practically?

The chief players in the system are human beings, other living creatures, and nature itself. The non-human elements are already mutually beneficial within the framework; it is the human factor that must reexamine its proper role and responsibility in the natural drama of life. Whether the play will end as comedy or tragedy depends upon human beings. If we humans are co-creative, correlative, symmetrical, and mutually beneficial, as all other living creatures are, then the flow of the story will take a pleasing shape. There will be harmony, order, beauty, and progress. All this means that the future of nature – as well as that of humanity – is very much dependent upon humanity's conscientious attitude and rational behavior. If we end in doom, it is we ourselves who are to blame. If we succeed and prosper continuously, it is also we ourselves we are to thank. We are the masters of our own existence and our own future, as well. If we master ourselves rationally, we will survive and prosper continuously. Otherwise, we face the prospect of being hauled into an abyss, to put it in Moltmann's words.

---

[26] For this reason, scholars are discussing the possibility of extending the theoretical scope of the theory to include the activities of large social establishments, such as the management of huge corporations or public organizations, Cf. J. Gleick, *Chaos: Making a New Science*, 83ff.

Of particular importance at this juncture is the colossal degree of sensitivity within chaotic systems. The radical change in Lorenz's final results stemmed from a negligible change in the initial conditions of the system. Indeed, the utter improbability of the shift warrants a look at the exact mathematical figures. The *Wilson Chronology of Science and Technology* puts the changed number in the eighth decimal place, i.e., .00000001 mathematically. Stewart says that the affected numbers in Lorenz's calculation consisted of the last three digits of the six decimal places usually entered in the computer, i.e., .000123.[27] That means Lorenz worked with the first three decimal numbers, i.e., .123, and deleted the last three numbers. Even at the number's face value, it's easy to see how negligible the change is. By all conventional standards, no one would pay serious attention to such a tiny discrepancy in their calculations. Lorenz was right to classify this shift as a "butterfly effect":

> The flapping of a single butterfly's wing today produces a tiny change in the state of the atmosphere. Over a period of time, what the atmosphere actually does diverges from what it would have done. So, in a month's time, a tornado that would have devastated the Indonesian coast doesn't happen. Or maybe one that wasn't going to happen, does.[28]

Taken literally, Lorenz's idea of a butterfly effect could cause more confusion than his idea of the chaotic system itself: the combined effect caused by the flapping wings of all the world's butterflies would turn out to be enormous. Such impact, of course, is not observed in the day-to-day experiences of weather. Lorenz used the analogy to draw a connection between an inconsequential event like the flapping of a single butterfly's wing and the overall unpredictability of the planet's weather system:

> The average person, seeing that we can predict the tides pretty well a few months ahead would say, "Why can't we do the same thing with the atmosphere? It's just a different system, the laws are about as complicated." But I realized that *any* physical system that behaved non-periodically would be unpredictable.[29]

---

[27] See I. Stewart, *Does God Play Dice?*, 141.

[28] *Ibid.*

[29] Cited by Stewart, *Ibid.*, 142.

The substantial change caused by the decimal figure in Lorenz's calculations demonstrates that the anthropogenic application of and input into the natural systems really does matter. Human beings have a responsibility to understand their symmetrical contribution to the natural balance with the utmost importance. If an uneven contribution occurs indefinitely, then the balance will be irretrievably broken, and humankind will find itself huddled together with nature in a single ship of disaster. This stresses once again the importance of attitude, behavior, and reasoning in humanity's relationship with its surroundings. Lorenz's experience shows, for instance, that driving a car more than necessary *really does matter*. The insatiable spirit of consumerism has terrible lasting effect. So, too, does the unbridled use of artificial fertilizers, the unrestricted polluting of rivers, the incessant release of greenhouse gases into the atmosphere. Prideful manufacturing and stockpiling of expensive weapons; arrogant neglect of nature; unnecessary killing; unrestricted extraction and burning of fossil fuels; unreasonable destruction of natural forests; uncalculated damming of rivers; uncontrolled increase in population: all of it *really does matter*.

These are only a few examples of the role human beings perform in the global drama of life. Everyone has an equal responsibility and obligation in curing the wounds and ills of nature. To forget one's role and behave irrationally is to add insult to nature's injury. The environment requires conscientious attention, care, and concern as much as humanity needs nature's mediation of God's providence and protection. If humankind turns a deaf ear to the deep cry of the natural order, if it ignores the injury, damage and oppression the environment suffers under humanity's merciless and reckless behavior, then nature will eventually enact its vengeance. Storms, floods, avalanche, and fires will rage out of control.

Recall once more the ethical maxim of Stoic philosophy: "live in harmony with nature." Nature has already bestowed enough lessons on humanity in the past; the question remains, whether we want to take these lessons to heart and live out our lives by conforming to their logical implications. Macroscopic systems have a great deal to offer, but so, too, do the natural properties of microscopic particles. The theoretical development and conceptual exposition of modern quantum mechanics therefore warrants an in-depth examination.

4.2 Chaos Theory and Quantum Mechanics

The idea and conceptual implications of Chaos Theory can be found within the framework of quantum mechanics. Like Chaos Theory, quantum theory (or, quantum mechanics) was introduced in the 20th century. In contrast to the classical model, quantum mechanics considers the properties, nature, and behavior of elementary particles in an atom or a molecule at the subatomic level.[30] Both classical physics and Newtonian and Einsteinian mechanics deal with massive and moving objects; quantum mechanics, on the other hand, mainly concentrates on the minute particles of the subatomic domains. The theory more or less began with the work of Max Planck, a German physicist and Nobel Laureate, in 1918. It later reached mathematic and conceptual maturity in about 1927.[31] Though scientists had already begun to explore subatomic phenomena by the beginning of the 20th century, exact knowledge of the internal structure and behavior of the atom had yet to be fully observed. A more detailed and satisfactory explanation concerning the existence of electrons was made by J. J. Thomson in 1897. It was over a decade later, however, in 1911, that Sir Ernest Rutherford proved that most of an atom's mass – and all of the positive charge – is concentrated at its center.[32] It took yet another two decades for James Chadwich to discover neutron particles (Cavendish Laboratory in England, 1932).[33]

Planck demonstrated in 1900 that light, X-rays, or other waves could

---

[30] Cf. Robert H. Dicke and James P. Wittke, *Introduction to Quantum Mechanics* (Reading, MA: Addison-Wesley Publishing Company, 1960), 3.

[31] See David C. Cassidy, *Uncertainty: The Life and Science of Werner Heisenberg* (New York: W. H. Freeman and Company, 1992), 91f. Heisenberg won the Nobel Prize in 1932. See Ulf Larsson, ed., *Cultures of Creativity: The Centennial Exhibition of the Nobel Prize*, trans. Daniel M. Olson (Canton, MA: Science History Publications, 2001), 216.

[32] Rutherford won the Nobel Prize for this finding in 1908. See Ulf Larsson, *Ibid.*, 217.

[33] Chadwich won the Nobel Prize for this finding in 1935. See Ulf Larsson, *Ibid.*, 216.

[34] Cf. S. Hawking, *A Brief History of Time*, 54.

[35] Light has several wavelengths, all varying in length. The shorter the wavelength is, the higher its energy is. Consequently, it is able to penetrate other objects more easily.

not be emitted at an arbitrary rate, but only in certain discrete packets which he called *quanta*, the plural of "quantum."[34] In other words, light, X-rays, or waves are emitted in indivisible units. Each quantum has a certain amount of energy. The greater the amount of energy there is, the higher the wave frequency (i.e., the shorter the wavelength).[35] The term "quantum" is derived from Planck's demonstration, and all subsequent proofs and theories about subatomic particles have collectively come to be called quantum mechanics.[36] In 1905, Einstein discovered the photoelectric effect, leading to the confirmation that light consists of a massless particle called a "photon," i.e., a quantum of light.[37] In his experiment, Einstein directed light to fall on a metal plate. He found that when the metal acquired energy from the light, it emitted radiation. Einstein was convinced of the photoelectric effect of the light on the plate and explained the phenomena as follows: light consists of photons, each of which carries within it a certain amount of energy. As photons come into contact with atoms (like those in the plate's metal), some of their energy is absorbed by electrons. When the electrons' energy gain reaches a critical point, they become stronger than the force that binds them to the atom's nucleus. The bond is broken, and the electron is ejected from the atom in the form of radiation.[38]

The Danish physicist Niels Bohr demonstrated an atomic structural model based on a hydrogen atom.[39] His discovery of the spectral lines of light, together with his model for atomic structure, helped scientists much in speculating on the structure and nature of subatomic particles. Because of Bohr's studies, the atom is no longer considered indivisible but is itself composed of smaller particles. All this combined research sparked enough motivation to explore the nature and behavior of reality at the subatomic

---

[36] Cf. Hawking, *A Brief History of Time*, 54ff.

[37] Einstein won the Nobel Prize for this finding in 1921. See Ulf Larsson, *Cultures of Creativity*, 216.

[38] Cf. *Encyclopedia Britannica*, vol. 11, 795.

[39] Bohr won the Nobel Prize for this discovery in 1922. See Ulf Larsson, *Cultures of Creativity*, 216.

[40] The difference between a particle and a wave is that a particle is a localized phenomenon which transports both mass and energy as it moves, whereas a wave is a de-localized phenomenon (something spread out across space) that carries energy but no mass. Cf. Cassidy, *Uncertainty*, 244.

level. This fervor eventually led to the development of quantum mechanics, even though all of the smaller subatomic particles were as yet undiscovered. From its very outset, the scientific analysis of quantum mechanics was burdened with ambiguity. Scientists were confused over the nature of light: was it a particle, or a wave?[40] Sometimes it behaves like the former, sometimes the latter.[41] The question of light's duality still lingers on in present scientific debate.[42] How one understands the nature of light is directly dependent upon theoretical orientation: scientists in the "particle" camp have found their assumption to "work" in experiments; but so, too, have those of the "wave" persuasion.[43] The relation between observer and observed thus plays a key role in the process.[44]

Another historical difficulty in analyzing quantum mechanics was Heisenberg's principle of uncertainty. Heisenberg states that one cannot precisely measure the position of a particle and its velocity simultaneously.[45] The more precisely one measures the position of the particle, the more inaccurately one will measure its velocity. Put the other way, the more accurately one measures the velocity of the particle, the more erroneously one will measure its position.[46]

---

[41] The French scientist De Broglie postulated the theory of light's dualistic nature, i.e., that light is both particle and wave. Consequently, he argued that all particles can be described either through wave equations or particle equations. For this De Broglie won the Nobel Prize in 1929. See Ulf Larsson, *Cultures of Creativity*, 216. Bohr later explained that the particle-like character and wave-like character of light are not two separate properties but are complementary to each other. See Cassidy, *Uncertainty*, 240-244.

[42] Hans Schwarz, *Creation*, 70f.

[43] In quantum mechanics, the formulation of the theory based on the idea of wave was known as wave mechanics; the theory based on the idea of particle was known as matrix mechanics. For more, see David, C. Cassidy, *Uncertainty*, 204-225.

[44] For more about the conceptual implications, see Ian G. Barbour, *Issues in Science and Religion*, 286-290.

[45] Cf. *Ibid.*, 228.

[46] For more details see *Ibid.*, 226-246.

The problem stems from the very nature of the system. Quantum mechanics deals with extremely small entities. It therefore has a natural disadvantage when it comes to precision and accuracy, as the technique and instruments used in measuring the particles impact the process itself. For instance, in order to find out the exact position of a particle within the atom, it must be illuminated. Some of the light waves will be scattered by the particle, consequently revealing its position. It will be impossible to determine the particle's position, however, if the light's wavelength is too long, because then the distance between the wave crests is too great.[47] A shorter wavelength is therefore necessary for accuracy. But here arises another problem. As mentioned above, the shorter wavelength carries a greater energy that helps accelerate the particle's velocity. So with a shorter wavelength, the *velocity* of the particle cannot be measured accurately. Time, trial, and error have revealed Heisenberg's principle to be a fundamental property of the world. Indeed, Hawking understands it as gospel truth:

> Moreover, this limit does not depend on the way in which one tries to measure the position or velocity of the particle, or on the type of particle: Heisenberg's uncertainty principle is a fundamental, inescapable property of the world.[48]

Heisenberg's principle shows that the nature and character of reality in the subatomic domains resembles that of Lorenz's chaotic system: the properties and behavior of particles at microscopic levels are characterized by complexity and unpredictability. If the nature of the fundamental building blocks of all matter is so indeterminate and unpredictable, then any assumption concerning the ability to predict precisely the physical state of the world at any given time is delusional. The conceptual and mathematical implications of quantum mechanics are evident in Hawking's theoretical stance on the matter:

> Since the structure of molecules and their reactions with each other underlie all of chemistry and biology, quantum mechanics allows us

---

[47] Cf. S. Hawking, *A Brief History of Time*, 54.

[48] *Ibid.*, 55. The following discussion will elucidate the view that Heisenberg's principle is independent of experimental limitation and lies at the fundamental center of reality.

[49] *Ibid.*, 60.

> in principle to predict nearly everything we see around us, within the limit set by the uncertainty principle. (In practice, however, the calculations required for systems containing more than a few electrons are so complicated that we cannot do them.)[49]

The rapid development of scientific investigation after the Second World War helped scientists discover even smaller particles than electrons, protons, and neutrons, as well as other particles in space like neutrinos, gravitons, bosons, etc.[50] The discovery of those particles as well as that of the "virtual particles" "antiproton, antineutron, anti-electron and antiparticle" paint the nature of reality at the subatomic level ever more complicated. Indeed, speculation concerning subatomic reality becomes so extremely difficult that even the "fixed" laws of nature lose their validity and applicability. It was once believed that the laws of nature obeyed the so-called three separate symmetries of C, P, and T. The "symmetry of C" means that the laws are uniform for all types of particles, both particles and antiparticles. The "symmetry of P" states that the laws are the same for every situation and its mirror image. And the "symmetry of T" holds that things will return to their original state or condition if the direction of their developmental process is reversed. Later on, observation proved that the laws of physics do not obey these three symmetries.[51] For instance, if all the particles of the universe were replaced with antiparticles, the universe would not continue to develop in the same way.[52] Moreover, if the developmental course of the universe were reversed (i.e., the reversal of time direction), it would in no way return to the point of the Big Bang in the same manner.[53]

In light of the above discussion, one can argue convincingly that reality in the subatomic realm is very similar to a chaotic system. As with the chaotic system, the structure, behavior, and properties of things at the

---

[50] For more detailed information about elementary particles, see S. Hawking, *ibid.*, 63-79; and also P. C. W. Davies & J. Brown, *Superstrings: A Theory of Everything?* (Cambridge: Cambridge University Press, 1988), 21-26.

[51] Cf. S. Hawking, *A Brief History of Time*, 77.

[52] Cf. *Ibid.*

[53] Cf. *Ibid.* 75.

[54] Cf. *Ibid.*, 75.

subatomic level are so complicated and unpredictable because many indeterminate factors involved. For instance, on the basis of the uncertainty principle, it is impossible to calculate exactly how much energy the quarks inside a proton (or a neutron, for that matter) will carry.[54] To make things more confusing, scientists are now divided into two camps concerning the nature of the quark: one group insists that quarks are point-like particles, whereas the other group is convinced that quarks are string-like entities with a shape of their own resembling a loop.[55] If quarks were actually a loop-like string, there would be enormous consequences for theoretical physics, allowing scientists to investigate and understand the nature of the world in much more detail than before. The problem, however, is that scientists have absolutely no means of verifying whether the extremely tiny quark is a point-like particle or a string-like entity.[56]

From a scientific point of view, every atom is considered to be a world of its own, because it has a particular structure and a fully functioning system. Eventually this hypothesis led to the formulation of "many-worlds and many-universes" theory.[57] If one regards every atom as a world of its own – even going so far as to speculate about the actual physical characteristics that make up of these countless atomic worlds – then the result is a rather perplexing picture, to say the least. Or, to offer a less harmonious illustration, if every atom is a chaotic system of its own, then there are limitless chaotic systems within the universe. That would make the structure of the universe more like a super-giant chaotic system containing myriads of chaotic systems within it. And here lies an inherent natural paradox: the contradictory appearance of reality at the subatomic level and at a macro-level. The ostensible existence of order and regularity in large-scale natural systems clashes completely with the complex and unpredictable nature of the subatomic. The intriguing question is: how is such a paradox possible within the uniform structure of the world? Is there

---

[55] P. C. W. Davies & J. Brown, *Superstrings*, 67-224.

[56] To verify experimentally whether quarks are point-like particles or string-like entities, one would need to construct a huge and powerful particle accelerator, the length of which would have to extend at least 10 light years. That means it would be almost as big as our solar system. See P.C.W. Davies and J. Brown, *Superstrings*, 171.

[57] Cf. Hugh Montefiore, *The Probability of God*, 35ff.

a logical temptation to equate this discrepancy with the so-called God-of-the-gaps? Or does it offer instead the opportunity to bring the metaphysical dimension fully into the discussion?

Not surprisingly, one finds that the unpredictability of reality in the subatomic realm has opened anew the discussion of divine intervention in the natural world processes. By all appearances, the same God who was driven from the world by classical physics has been invited by quantum mechanics to return and resume his intervention in natural phenomena. To put it another way, Einstein's God "who never plays dice" seems to have taken up the game if quantum mechanics rules the show. That was precisely the reason why Einstein was hesitant to accept the logic of quantum mechanics. He argued instead that there might be some as yet unobserved natural causes in the world that cause subatomic particles to appear and behave unpredictably.[58] He believed that at some point in the future science would be able to disclose these causes. Given the state of scientific advancement at his time, Einstein was not wrong in his reasoning. All this implies that the world of modern scientific reasoning does not totally exclude the possibility of the role of God in nature. Some see the divine presence in the idea of special providence; yet, whatever implications a metaphysical explanation may have for others, scientists have little interest in it. Accordingly, they will always be searching for a scientific answer to the paradox – and indeed, there could very well be such an answer within the mathematical mystery at the heart of the chaos system.

4.3   Miracle and Chaos

That scientists have uncovered new mystery in and under the chaotic system; that there can be an order beneath the superficial disorder, a harmony in the current of chaos, regularity underlying irregularity, symmetry out of asymmetry – is utterly enthralling. [59] One could call this enigma "a ghost in the chaos", similar to "the ghost in the atom"[60] that scientists used to describe the astonishingly wonderful behavior of particles

---

[58] M. W. Worthing, *God, Creation, and Contemporary Physics*, 50.

[59] See J. Gleick, *Chaos: Making a New Science*, 4-7.

[60] This is the title Paul Davies has given to one of his books.

at the subatomic level. Lorenz himself saw hints of this mystery with his experimental discovery of the chaotic weather system. Spellbound by the utter incredulity of the consequences of the decimal shift, Lorenz continued calculating the weather on the computer; this time, however, he was calculating possible results for convection, changing the variables several times and initiating the program repeatedly. To match his intentions, he used only the three variables of Saltzman for his equation and allowed it to repeat 3000 times. To his surprise, he discovered that a somewhat symmetrical, two-lobed figure had formed on the x-y plane. A nearly symmetrical figure had emerged out of asymmetrical states; technically speaking, it represented a mysterious and unforeseen attractor. Hence, this phenomenon has later come to be known as the "Lorenz attractor".[61]

Another miraculous and chaotic phenomenon was observed by a Harvard economics professor, Hendrik S. Houthakker, and a Yale University mathematics professor and IBM fellow, Benoit Mandelbrot. Houthakker wanted to know the nature of the price fluctuations of cotton, so he gathered the relevant data and entered it in his computer. He expected the price fluctuation over the long term to be more or less steady, but in a short term to be random. Houthakker's data failed to match his expectations: there were too many large jumps, most price changes were small, and the ratio of the two fluctuations was not as high as he expected. The results did not square with the pattern of distribution because the distribution did not drop off quickly. Houthakker tried again and again without any. Later on, Mandelbrot contacted Houthakker and learned of his difficulty. The problem piqued Mandelbrot's interest, and he attempted to solve it himself. He collected data as far back as 1900 and re-entered it into the computer. To his wonder, he found an amazing consistency in the sequence of price fluctuations. Gleick reports Mandelbrot's findings as follows:

> The numbers that produced aberrations from the point of view of normal distribution produced symmetry from the point of view of scaling. Each particular price change was random and unpredictable. But the sequence of changes was independent of scale: curves for daily price changes and monthly price changes matched perfectly.

---

[61] For more information, see Stewart, *Does God Play Dice?* 134-139.

[62] James Gleick, *Chaos: Making a New Science*, 86.

Incredibly, analyzed Mandelbrot's way, the degree of variation had remained constant over a tumultuous sixty-year period that saw two World Wars and a depression.[62]

Given Mandelbrot's findings, one can imagine how disordered and disarrayed the price fluctuation sequence would be over this sixty-year period. By conventional standards, no one would ever expect to find any mathematical uniformity in such a long and chaotic sequence. But it did exist, that much is certain. Mandelbrot demonstrated that there can be order beneath the superficial appearance of chaotic chance; in other words, one could say that it is order in the guise of chaos.

Mysteries of this kind occur readily in other natural phenomena: for example, in the male/female ratio of the population of a large society. A number of babies are born in any given society daily. Some of them will be boys and some girls; but what one can say for certain is that the number of boys and girls will never be equal. Neither will the births take place in the same living quarters. Some of them will be born in one building, some in another, etc. Suppose that someone tries to find out the ratio of males to females by drawing lines on the map between the birthplaces of individual babies of the opposite sex for a given amount of time. What picture will emerge from this venture? One way or another, the picture will never be a simple one. The lines will crisscross each other at several points, and the crisscrossing itself will repeat and multiply indefinitely. The end result of the experiment will be a total mess, because the labyrinth of lines will overlap again and again. From a geometrical point of view, one could never hope to find any regularity or orderliness within such total disarray. The reality is, however, that such an underlying equilibrium (regularity) *does exist* in and under totally disconnected natural phenomena (irregularity). Somehow, the male/female proportion of a population happens to achieve complete balance over a certain period of time. This equal matching of male and female is a marvelous example of a regular equilibrium underlying a gross irregularity (i.e., the haphazard births of boys and girls within a population).

Even in the distant past, people – especially natural theologians –

---

[63] John D. Barrow, *Theory of Everything,* 129f.

observed this wondrous yet natural trend in their midst and took it as a sign of God's mysterious providence.[63] It is easy to imagine the consequences such an absence of underlying regularity would have on the growth of a population. If men outnumbered women greatly, there would constantly be war between individual men as well as between nations; for, given these circumstances, if there were no war to curb the male population, then humans would have to live as animals. Morality would collapse, and there would be no sound foundation upon which to build human civilization. Under these circumstances, human civilization would never have progressed to the point that it is today. On the other hand, if women greatly outnumbered men, then civilization would be held in check, because human beings would not have enough free time for scientific observation and systematic contemplation. Individual men would have to marry a number of women; and although no serious problems would arguably arise from this trend directly, difficulty would stalk in through the back door. Caring and feeding the numerous children born to them, parents would be terribly busy all the time. Given all of these possibilities, neither option has a positive outlook. This would appear quite a minor matter for some, or perhaps sound ridiculous and stupid; from a moral perspective, however, its implications for human civilization are profound. A philosophical education provides the capacity to hold an *a posteriori* perspective, i.e., the ability to see the logical progression of events by looking back over the past from the present. Without a series of specific conditions in the past, the situation at present would not be as it is. The concept of "condition" thus comes into view, the importance of which is emphasized strongly by both scientists and philosophers. Here one cannot easily ignore the argument that the equilibrium (i.e., underlying regularity

---

[64] Cf. John D. Barrow, *Theories of Everything*, 130ff. Instead, Barrow finds his explanation in the Darwinian theory. He argues that random processes possess the responsive capacity for such balancing in natural phenomena. It is interesting to note that instead of referring to DNA, he refers to Darwin's theory of evolution. One must wait and see whether or not the equal birth rate of males and females in a population can be explained genetically in the future. At present, it is certain that one can change the gender of the baby genetically in the early stage of its development in the mother's womb. What would happen if every couple decided the sex of their unborn child in the embryonic stage instead of leaving it to the natural mechanism?

in the midst of uncertainty) in the male and female population was the most important natural condition required for humanity to arrive at its current stage of civilization.

Scientists do not usually want to claim a theologically-oriented perception of natural population balance;[64] however, sometimes one can glean profound pieces of providence from the simple experiences of daily life. Great scientists and scholars of the past, for instance, saw overwhelming insight in quotidian human habits, like the power of steam from a kettle boiling on an open fire. Jesus himself used simple things in the surrounding environment to illustrate his message. These lessons hold such deep wisdom and illustrative power that they easily touch the hearts and grip the lives of his listeners.

Harmony exists within the turmoil of chaos. A song sung by a choir, for example, has four different parts: soprano, alto, tenor, and bass. Each part has its own pattern of notation, and the singers sing the song according to their respective tune-notations. Were one to draw a graph to mark the "path" each of the parts move along throughout the course of the song, the four routes would never be uniform or linear. Each part will vibrate up and down according to the ups and downs of the notation. If all four parts were drawn together with a single keynote as a common starting point, then the lines will inevitably crisscross each other unevenly along the path. The interlacing of the lines means the direction of the tunes is chaotic. But one knows from experience that there is equilibrium within a choir. It is this accord – quite literally, this harmony – that causes a choir or a song to gain popularity and enthralls those who hear it.[65]

Natural terrestrial phenomena are like choral music. For many, natural phenomena appear totally chaotic. The blowing of the wind in any and all directions, the uneven formation of clouds in the sky, the sporadic flooding of lakes and rivers, the simultaneous occurrences of droughts in some places and torrential rains in other places, the existence of a variety of animals and plants both harmful and benevolent: all will cause confusion. And yet poets and composers both continue to find a harmony in the midst

---

[65] For more about this type of miracle in music, see I. Stewart, *Does God Play Dice?*, 156-164.

of this chaos. W.A. Mozart, for example, heard the sweet melody in the deep silence beneath nature's superficial ramblings. And there is no better illustration in ancient poetry of the stark quality of creation's wonders than the Psalmist of the Bible.

Due to the rapid and significant development of science in the 20th century, human beings are able to study and uncover those mysteries within natural systems.[66] If powerful computers used to monitor weather systems had never been invented, then it would be impossible to map out this chaotic system and unravel its mystery. Lorenz's advantage was that he had had a well-equipped laboratory, enabling him to calculate long and complicated equations. Another scientific contribution that influenced the understanding of chaotic systems was fractal geometry. Chaos Theory and fractal geometry emerged at almost at the same point in time. Fractal geometry was invented by Mandelbrot and became widely known in the 1970s.[67] Although Lorenz had already written about chaos systems a decade earlier (1963), it took several years for the idea to be widely recognized within the scientific community. Had these two new ideas not been discovered during the period, any talk about "mystery within chaos" would have no basis. Given the coincidental emergence of these two ideas and the significance of their combined contributions, one can logically infer that there may be more laws of nature to be discovered. Consideration of the term "miracle" in conjunction with these laws of nature would certainly be appropriate.

Scientists are usually of the opinion that every natural event can be explained according to the laws of nature.[68] When an event cannot be thus explained, it is either discarded as improbable or regarded as a miracle. Understanding "miracle" in this manner is relative in that it is directly connected to the theoretical and explanatory capacity of the laws of nature. The question once again arises: has humanity discovered all the laws of nature in the universe? The answer is obviously "no," even though

---

[66] For more about later developments in the analysis of chaotic systems, see William L. Ditto and Louis M. Pecora, "Mastering Chaos," 62-68.

[67] Cf. I. Stewart, *Does God Play Dice?*, 215f.

[68] In this day and age, scientists are discussing the limit to the applicability of natural laws, see J. D. Barrow, *Theory of Everything*, 208ff.

humankind has been able to make quantum-leap advancements in technology and scientific theory. This means that the possibility of miracle is not totally prohibited according to existing scientific laws. Miracle is still open to the future, just as the laws of science themselves remain open.

Many of the miracles reported in the Bible are discarded as improbable when viewed alongside modern scientific laws. Their rejection is due to the fact that they stand in direct contradiction to the theoretical and empirical observation of natural laws. Jesus' walking on water, for instance, is a prime example. In light of the logical implications of the existing laws of nature, one would have to refute such a claim. But one can concurrently argue against this "limited" view by theorizing that there may be an opposite law to explain such a phenomenon. This probability is especially high given the reversed and opposite reality within chaotic systems. Many oriental religions believe in the existence of an inner energy called "chi" or "qi," and human access to this inner energy through systematic practices is well recognized, even in highly industrialized nations like Japan. *Chi* is more of a secular nature and can be realized by methodical focus of the mind and soul.[69] Bodhisattva is another important concept in the religious traditions of Asia.[70] One can attain Bodhisattva (i.e., enlightenment) status through proper and strict religious practice. Tradition holds that hermits living in the solitude of forests or caves who attain Bodhisattva status through devout meditation obtain extraordinary spiritual power to foresee things far into the future. This focused clairvoyance is a result of being in a full union with God; and the ability to walk on water is not unheard of in these traditions, either.[71] The existence and channeling of this inner spiritual power has yet to be subjected to scientific analysis. Given enough time and resources

---

[69] See Lindsay Jones, Editor in Chief, *Encyclopedia of Religion*, 2nd ed., vol. 11 (Detroit: Macmillan Reference USA, 2005), 7544f. Also see Yasuo Yuasa, "Modern Scientific Paradigm and the Discovery of the Inner Cosmos," in *Cosmos.Life.Religion: Beyond Humanism*, 453-472.

[70] See Lindsay Jones, *Encyclopedia of Religion*, vol. 2, 996-1000.

[71] *Ibid.* Also see R. Balasubramanian, "The Hindu Perspective of Man and the Cosmos," in *Cosmos " Life " Religion: Beyond Humanism*, 320-332; also see Koshiro Tamaki, "Cosmic Life: Based on Whole-Personality-Thinking against Objective Thinking," in *Cosmo " .Life " Religion: Beyond Humanism*, 201-218.

dedicated to the study and of such phenomena, new laws of nature could very well be uncovered, perhaps even a logical explanation for walking on water.

The same sort of possibilities arises with the miracle of healing. Jesus healed people here and there on various occasions during his three-year ministry. Past scholarship rebuffed many of these healing accounts as myths on scientific grounds. Taking Chaos Theory into account, however, one can logically pose the question as to whether or not healing miracles can be scientifically justified according to natural processes. Given humanity's unconsummated knowledge of existing scientific laws, let alone those yet to be found in the future, the ready refusal of such miracles displays neither a proper spiritual attitude nor a professional academic approach. According to modern psychoanalytical discoveries, one can argue that such miracles can – and do – take place. The power of love is not to be taken lightly, especially given its dynamical effect. Everyone knows something of this power, but more often than not it is simply taken for granted. To contemplate the "power of love" from a scientific point of view is almost unheard of; and yet, can it not be said that love exerts its effects in a manner similar to magnetic force? Understood in this way, one can talk about the dynamical field of love's power. Those things falling into this dynamic field will feel its effects, and accordingly acquire a certain direction and momentum. One could even offer the name "agapodynamism" to this dynamical field of love and the nature of its effect. If such an agapodynamic field exists, then one can explain Jesus' healing miracles by speculating that the patients brought into the field of Jesus' agapodynamism, i.e., into his presence, felt the power of his love acting upon their life. The immediate effect was a dramatic psychological impact, followed by the physical and/ or mental healing of the patients. Modern depth psychology theory and Jung's theory of synchronicity even discuss such "miraculous" phenomena in modern psychoanalytical fields.[72] Yasuo Yuasa (1925-2005), late professor at Osaka University, discusses Jung's idea of a psychic power for natural healing, latent within the human subconscious.

---

[72] Cf. Yasuo Yuasa, "Modern Scientific Paradigms and the Discovery of the Inner Cosmos," in *Cosmos " Life " Religion: Beyond Humanism*, 458-466.

[73] *Ibid.*, 462.

> The role of [the] psychoanalyst is only to discover the symptoms
> and provide hints for the patient to draw on this natural healing
> process. The natural healing power may be an unknown natural
> power latent within a human being that can be considered in
> terms of both mind and body; it can also be understood as a kind
> of energy that sustains life.[73]

Yuasa's view could explain the Gospel healing accounts according to the
natural healing power residing in the subconscious of the patient. This
dormant, natural ability may have been activated by the power of Jesus'
love, thereby leading to the actual physical healing of the patient.
Miraculous healing thus remains a scientific possibility, even in the age of
modern medicine.

All the above mysteries found within chaotic systems could be
described as miracles, even in the strictest sense of the term itself, because
the cause of some of the mysteries simply have no satisfactory scientific
explanation. For instance, the equilibrium alongside the irregular births
of males and females is hard to explain scientifically. One can even argue
that the existence and working of the laws of nature is a consequence of
God's special providential activities. Such reasoning is fully consistent with
Wolfhart Pannenberg's understanding of contingency. His view concerning
how contingency relates with the laws of nature warrants further analysis.

4.4   Pannenberg's Understanding of Contingency

Wolfhart Pannenberg assumes that every conceivable reality in the world
does not originate of itself but is the result of a divine creative act. This
means that every aspect of temporal reality is directly contingent upon
God:

> The theological affirmation that the world of nature proceeds from
> an act of divine creation implies the claim that the existence of the
> world as a whole and of all its parts is contingent. The existence of
> the whole world is contingent in the sense that it needs not be at all.

---

[74] See Wolfhart Pannenberg, "The Doctrine of Creation and Modern Science,"
in *Toward a Theology of Nature: Essays on Science and Faith*, ed. Ted Peters
(Louisville: Westminster/John Knox Press, 1993), 34.

[75] See Pannenberg, "Contingency and Natural Laws," in *Toward a Theology of
Nature*, 76.

> It owes its existence to the free activity of divine creation. So does
> every single part of the world.[74]

Pannenberg argues that according to the Israelite understanding of God, the experience of reality is characterized primarily by contingency, particularly the contingency of occurrence. New and unforeseen events take place constantly, and the ancient Hebrews experienced them as works of almighty God.[75] According to this belief, it is not only isolated events in history that are wonderful and miraculous, but all occurrences in the cosmos. Based on this concept of contingency, Pannenberg explains the appropriateness of Christian faith and its relation to the future:

> Only on the presupposition of such an understanding of reality
> is it meaningful, for the Israelite and for the Christian heir of the
> Israelite tradition, to pray. Furthermore, on this basis faith
> appears as the behavior that is, in the last analysis, alone
> appropriate to reality. For the fact that again and again new events
> take place means that one cannot render a final judgment
> concerning the context in which present and past events and
> figures stand and from which their significance is to be
> determined: only the future will reveal what is "in it."[76]

Understanding reality in terms of such a contingency tends to be contradictory to the apparent existing order in nature and nature's laws. Pannenberg argues accordingly that ancient Israel was aware of permanent order in nature as well as in human society. But these orders were conceived as dependent on the contingency of the divine will, not only in view of their origin but also in view of their continuance.[77] Concerning these regularities in nature, Pannenberg writes:

> Nature's regularity can be compared with positive legislation, whose
> laws fundamentally permit of exceptions and can be changed by the
> legislator, rather than with the idea of a law of nature that permits of
> no exceptions and is unchangeable.[78]

---

[76] *Ibid.*

[77] *Ibid.*, 76f.

[78] *Ibid.*

[79] *Ibid.*, 97.

Pannenberg's perception regarding the regularities in nature tends to stand in direct contrast to the general scientific rule regarding the laws of nature. Pannenberg himself is well aware of this point. As far he is concerned regarding order in nature, there is no tension between a) regularity in terms of contingency and b) scientific understanding of nature's laws in the mathematical sense. According to Pannenberg, the laws of nature are the abstractions of regularities from divinely contingent phenomena in the world for methodological reasons.[79]

It is clear that for Pannenberg the laws of nature are not some sort of built-in programs in the structure of the world whose forms and functions are eternally valid and unchangeable. The seemingly permanent character of the laws of nature reveals nothing about their intrinsic structure. Rather, they are descriptions of the connections of contingent occurrences. In the Israelite understanding of history, however, the connection of occurrences in the world is not constituted by human action in history. This connection is instead established by God through His actions in the world. This conviction was fashioned in ancient Israel through the knowledge that Yahweh explicitly directed Israel's future through promise and fulfillment; therefore, Israel experienced the contingent events of its history as the way in which Yahweh held to His promises.[80] If laws of nature are indeed descriptions of overall patterns within the greater context of contingencies, as well as of the connection between contingencies, the question then becomes: how can the permanent character of natural laws be understood and interpreted alongside the perception of contingencies as divine activities? Pannenberg's answer is that it is the faithfulness of God in His relationship with the world that shapes the basic character of uniformity out of the creation's contingencies.[81] Concerning this relationship between divine faithfulness and the uniformity of contingent occurrences (or uniformity of the laws of nature), Pannenberg writes:

> To that extent the faithfulness of God " who, as Israel's experience of God saw it in its history, in all contingency of his acting

---

[80] *Ibid.*, 85.

[81] *Ibid.*, 109.

[82] *Ibid.*, 109-110.

nevertheless adheres to earlier election and thus manifests in such a way his identity with himself repeatedly " can be asserted as the condition for the fact that forms of process originate at all that can be described by laws of nature. On the basis of the faithfulness of God, by his self-identification in the sequence of his contingent acting, it becomes understandable why the contingent events do not simply accumulate without connection but show the unique inclination to "latch" into solid, regularly repeated forms of process. Only in this way, that continuity of occurrences seems to originate which opens up for us the possibility of numbering arrangements and thus the possibility of formulating regular connections.[82]

There is some logical substance to Pannenberg's view of contingency, even though some would take it as too conceptually formulated. His assertion that the laws of nature are descriptions of regularity within contingent phenomena deserves to be given proper attention and discussion. His position on contingency can also be seen as a conceptual complement to what the physicist Paul Davies says concerning dependability in the operation of the laws of nature.[83] At present, scientists like John D. Barrow speak of the need for a deeper conceptual analysis of the laws of nature. Barrow points out that there is a difference between the outcome of the laws of nature and the laws of nature themselves.[84] He further contends that people have often regarded the outcome of the laws of nature as identical with the laws themselves.[85] In reality, argues Barrow, this is not the case. The laws of nature are expressed in the form of mathematical equations to deal with data from natural phenomena.[86] Epistemologically speaking, these mathematical formulae or equations are not the laws of nature themselves but the outcome of the laws.[87] Though one can have precise knowledge of the working of these equations through theory and

---

[83] For Davies' assertion about the dependability in the operation of natural laws, see Paul Davies, *The Mind of God*, 195.

[84] See John D. Barrow, *Theory of Everything*, 115.

[85] *Ibid.*

[86] Cf. *ibid.*, 115f.

[87] *Ibid.*, 181-188.

[88] See *Physics Today: The World Book Encyclopedia of Science*, vol. 2, 141; and also Davies and Brown, *Superstrings*, 16f.

practice, this knowledge does not categorically lead to exact comprehension of the actual laws. For example, the Newtonian gravity equation has long been recognized as a norm when it comes to the question of gravity; but centuries after Newton, scientists learned through Einstein's theory of relativity that the Newtonian gravity equation is not synonymous with the exact nature of the law of gravity. For that matter, neither is Einstein's theory of general relativity itself perfect or complete.[88] It continues to gain wider acceptance and popularity because of its ability to describe, calculate, and predict natural phenomena on a larger scale, i.e., on a cosmic level.

From an epistemological point of view, the reliability and dependability of mathematics must be called into question. Mathematics is ultimately a product of human reasoning without sufficient empirical experience. Einstein himself developed a suspicious attitude toward the nature of mathematics:

> How can it be that mathematics, being after all a product of human thought which is independent of experience, is so admirably appropriate to the objects of reality? Is human reason, then, without experience, merely by taking thought, able to fathom the properties of real things? In my opinion the answer to this question is, briefly, this: As far as the laws of mathematics refer to reality, they are not certain; and as far as they are certain, they do not refer to reality.[89]

What we can know for sure is the ontological character of the laws of nature. In terms of ontology, the question becomes: are the laws of nature permanent and everlasting in nature and essence? To this one must simply answer, "No," because the laws of nature are very much dependent upon numerous other physical conditions, which are not permanently fixed but susceptible to various contingencies. The present physical conditions of the world, for example, could undergo extreme change because of nuclear war. Such a radical and violent environmental impact could very well forever alter the way environmental processes operate. The most probable consequence of an all-out nuclear war is the complete disarray of biological processes (if not the total extinction of most organisms) due to huge levels

---

[89] Cited by Hans Schwarz in his *Creation*, xi.

[90] Cf. *Physics Today: The World Book Encyclopedia of Science*, 141. Also see Hans Schwarz, *Creation*, 36f.

of radioactivity. In a similar fashion, scientists claim that it is impossible to trace the origins and developmental course of the universe, as there have been so many drastic physical changes in its development up to the present. Even if one were able to pinpoint the initial origin of the universe, the eventual outcome would be a veritable dead end, a point of singularity where the laws of nature are not applicable because the physical conditions are so extremely different.[90]

In light of this scientific discussion, one cannot easily dismiss Pannenberg's view that the laws of nature are descriptions of regularity within contingent phenomena. His conception of contingency provides an answer to the question of observable orderliness in the world. Viewed in light of Chaos Theory, the regularity and order in the world on the macro-level could be attributed to the providential activities of God, a clear demonstration of God's gracious work for all creatures.

4.5 The World as a Living Miracle

The human race owes boundless thanks to God for the lives of ingenious scientists whose theories, discoveries, and inventions have disclosed the wonders of nature to the world. Without this God-given source of human insight, many scientific facts would have otherwise remained natural taboos with superstitious implications. Human ingenuity has enabled civilization to set itself free from the enslaving powers of nature. The nature of the relationship between science and religion has regularly changed with successive stages of past technological development. At the dawn of human civilization, observation of nature produced a potent religious worldview. Various ancient cultures bear witness to this worship of nature,

---

[91] J. D. Barrow argues that the holistic worldview in Eastern cultures made it difficult for science to develop there. For more see his *Theory of Everything*, 13.

[92] Modern scientists like Decartes, Pascal, Kepler, Leibniz, Newton, Boyle, Faraday, and Maxwell were very religious men. The implication and significance of their ground-breaking works in science should never be forgotten. See Thaveedu Aruldoss, "Christian Faith in Dialogue with Science and Technology," in David C. Ratke, ed., *Theology at the Beginning of the 3rd Millennium in a Global Context* (Frankfurt am Main: Peter Lang, 1999), 201-209; and also J. D. Barrow, *Theory of Everything*, 14.

[93] See Hans Schwarz, *Creation*, 5.

especially the ancient Hellenistic world. With the emergence of monotheistic religion and its stark emphasis upon direct special revelation, nature became a mere cultural object, and the process of secularization was irreversibly in motion.[91]

In later centuries the belief in a self-revealing God and a secularized worldview entwined with each other, thereby laying the necessary foundation for the development of modern science. The effect of this dual influence is conspicuous in the lives of many modern scientists.[92] It is especially vivid in the life-story of Isaac Newton, one of the most influential modern thinkers. Newton's deep religious belief and its conceptual implications for his scientific work have often been emphasized.[93] Yet Newton remains but one small example of an overarching paradigm: the Judeo-Christian worldview together with the analytical skill and philosophical tradition of the Greco-Roman tradition provided the congenial environment and the necessary epistemological tools for science to develop.[94] The influence of the Judeo-Christian ethos is quite visible, for instance, in Einstein's oft-quoted religious aphorism: "God does not play dice."

Although Newton's faith-grounded depiction of the world tended to strengthen the religion/science relationship in the initial phases of modern science, subsequent developments took a U-turn and thoroughly opposed faith-based principles. The picture of the world itself changed markedly. No longer mysterious and puzzling, it was simple and scientifically explainable in every minute detail.[95] Consequently, the portrait of the world

---

[94] Cf. Barrow, *Theory of Everything,* 12ff.

[95] Here one calls to mind the above remarks of Laplace.

[96] The rise of communism can be considered an example of pushing God into the background, whereas Deism is one of confining God to an amorphous heaven.

[97] Thinkers like French physician and philosopher Julian Offray de la Mettrie, German naturalist Paul Heinrich Dietrich von Holbach, German philosopher Ludwig Feuerbach, materialistic thinkers Karl Marx and Friedrich Engels, and British empiricist David Hume are all representative of this trend. The works of these intellectuals have contributed much toward the divergence between religion and science in modern time.

was, as mentioned previously, that of a well-designed and -constructed machine. Every knot of earlier puzzles concerning the character of the world appeared to be untied once and for all. God was no longer needed, as far as the origin and disposition of the world were concerned. Accordingly, the divine was either pushed into the background or exiled to a heavenly abode.[96] The religion/science divorce had thus begun, its root anchored firmly in a mechanical understanding of the world. Subsequent developments in various fields of scientific investigation, especially in the 19th and the early period of the 20th century, only tended to support the mechanistic worldview. Indeed, the emergence of radical materialism and Darwinism further strengthened the already widespread admiration of the mechanistic worldview.[97]

Even the field of social science, which focused its study on the nature of the human mind, turned out to be less than supportive of religious faith. Human disposition, attitude, mentality, and behavior were exhaustively examined, disclosed, and settled by the famous theories of the psychologist Sigmund Freud.[98] The same can be said of progress in the medical field. The enormous strides made in the fields of anatomy, physiology, ethology, and pathology, as well as in therapeutic methods: all tended to convey the idea that the biological make-up, behavior, and work of human life were set in stone and thoroughly predictable. Life itself appeared simplistic and easily explainable scientifically. All achievements in scientific fields encouraged the growing sense of unbridled human self-esteem, and consequently an unlimited optimism in social and cultural advancement became the atmospheric aura of the age. Ever gradually the diverging trend grew stronger, never effectively checked or turned back. The chasm between religion and science seemed insurmountable, and the two disciplines looked irreconcilable.

---

[98] Freud's works on psychological analysis based on his clinical findings were a destructive blow for religious faith in the early part of this period. His books *The Future of an Illusion,* (1961), *The Interpretations of Dreams* (1953), *Essays on the Theory of Sexuality* (1953), *Totem and Taboo* (1955), and *Moses and Monotheism* (1960) contain many features that had profound implications for religious faith and teachings.

Rapid scientific developments as well as the disastrous events after World War II, however, changed much of the human perception of worldly reality in the later half of the 20th century. The great economic depression in 1929 and the ugly, destructive experiences of the two World Wars badly scarred humanity's self-esteem and unlimited optimism. The casualties and destruction of the two World Wars were so substantial that many European nations had to start life again from the ruins of the war. It would not be an exaggeration to say that humankind's spirit itself was buried in the destruction's debris. Whether or not the democratic political system could survive and prosper again was highly questionable. To make things more puzzling, the world, and especially Europe, was divided into two directly opposite political camps. The first was an absolute totalitarian system encapsulated in the saccharine ideological jargon of communism, and the second was a free democratic system imbued with problems and challenges of all kinds. In such a situation it was quite imaginable that one could hardly have hope for the future. Prospects looked bleak and unpromising; everything appeared gloomy and grim, both politically and economically. Humanity's self-esteem and optimism themselves appeared to be the cause of any war.

In addition, scientific developments in the twentieth century dealt a severe blow to humanity's earlier perception of the world picture. With the formulation of quantum theory and the subsequent speculative success in quantum physics, humankind's earlier understanding of the working of the laws of nature came under fire. The subsequent discovery of detailed atomic structure plus the theoretical success of quantum mechanics had turned the whole previous worldview upside down. The old image of the world as machine could no longer be upheld. The world system no longer appeared to be simple, determinate, or easily explainable. It was once again mysterious, indeterminate, and unpredictable. The old ghosts of insecurity

---

[99] For more about Jung's view, see his *The Psychology of the Unconscious* (1916), *The Unconscious in the Normal and Pathological Mind* (1928), *Psychology and Religion* (1938), and *Jung On Synchronicity and the Paranormal*, sel. and intro. Roderick Main (London: Routledge, 1997). See also *The Collected Works of Jung*, Bollingen Series, vols. 1-20 (New York/Princeton, N. J.: Pantheon, 1953-1979).

[100] For instance, H. J. Eysenck's sharp criticism of Freud's psychoanalysis in his *Decline and Fall of the Freudian Empire* (Harmonsworth: Viking, 1985).

had come to life again. New theories and experiences such as Chaos Theory and the ecological crisis tended to reopen the door and allow uncertainty to waltz into the room. The question became whether the ghosts would remain or be chased away by newer scientific findings.

In social science, Carl Gustav Jung's groundbreaking work on depth psychology based on experimental observations revealed new facets of human psychology.[99] Many of Freud's theories and views were challenged and in some cases proved to be untenable by the work of others.[100] Jung's discovery that there exists a close link between our religious faith and our psychological wholeness, for example, runs quite contrary to Freud's negative view and interpretation of religious faith. Jung's concept of synchronicity and depth psychology bring to light more insight into the inner mysterious realm of human psychology. The inquiry as to how the human mind and soul are related and work together exhibits new wonders inside the inner world of human thought. Further findings of this wondrous interaction between the inner and outer cosmos of the human being make things more enigmatic than before. The human mind itself becomes a universe of its own, every bit as mysterious as the physical universe itself.[101]

In the biological field, the picture is not so different from others discussed above. Scientific breakthroughs in biology are as breathtaking and profound as the achievements in other fields. The discovery of DNA and how it works in life bears witness to this wonder. With the finding of DNA, everything seems settled; ironically, however, it is exactly through DNA itself that new mystery in the natural system becomes present. The failure to produce life by combining DNA and proteins in the laboratory demonstrates that life is truly a mystery.[102] With the help of a powerful microscope, human beings are now able to observe in minute detail the course of a life from the very moment of fertilization to the final seconds

---

[101] See Yasuo Yuasa, "Modern Scientific Paradigms and the Discovery of the Inner Cosmos," 453-472.

[102] See the discussion in chapter 3.

[103] See Kazuo Murakami, "Genetics and Life," in *Cosmos —Life—Religion: Beyond Humanism*, 246.

before death. New studies of the life process demonstrate how mysterious and confounding it really is. The Japanese geneticist Murakami vividly describes the enigmatic progression of life as follows:

> Moreover, although a human body consists of trillions of cells, its very origin is a single fertilized egg. This egg repeats its twofold division many times over, thereby creating many organs and eventually a whole human body. Although it begins from one cell, as the growth of the original cell advances, it branches into other entirely different cells like blood corpuscles or internal organs. Why is it that entirely different organs are thus formed, when the DNA in the different cells remains the same even after differentiation. It is thought

that when a cell is divided, most of the unnecessary genes become inactive. However, little is known about this facet, either. Furthermore, humans have a higher functional plane of spirituality such as consciousness and mind. Relating to this spiritual function, nothing has yet been explained at the level of the molecule.[103]

The discussion in this chapter has demonstrated that, far from settling the riddles of life and the world, modern science has proven more and more how mysterious and wondrous life and all natural systems really are. It would not be wrong to say that the world is quintessentially a living miracle. It looks as if the religious faith which seemed totally destroyed and buried by the early stages of scientific development has now been resurrected and resuscitated by subsequent progress. Is this the beginning of the convergence between religious faith and scientific endeavor? If so, the question is how it will transpire in the future. And the answer is best left to the future itself.

Chapter 5

Biblical and Theological Complement

Ps. 89:11-12 is a powerful hymn of praise to God for his wondrous creative works:

> Heaven is yours, the earth also is yours
>
> The productive land and what fills it
>
> You yourself have founded them
>
> The north and the south
>
> You yourself have created them

Tabor and Hermon

In your name they cry out joyfully.

A reflection of nature's ecosystem would not be complete without proper contemplation of the biblical witness of God's providence. The Bible does not provide the kind of empirical report of providence in nature like those described in the preceding chapters. There are several allusions, however, in biblical teachings both positive and negative, from which springs insightful and useful information. These teachings together form an overarching conceptual stance on ecological realities, a biblical environmental ethic that is indispensable for healing the broken relationship between human beings and nature.

5.1   God's Providence in Nature in the Old Testament

The presence of and distinction between a *general* and a *special* providence is a common and pervasive theme in the Old Testament. Both aspects of divine providence are easily discernible in the convictions and customs of Israel. The tradition of offering thanksgiving for God's general providence appears often in the Old Testament. Moreover, the concept of covenant stands at the very center of the Jewish faith. The essence of "covenant" in the Old Testament narrative is God's promises and his determination to fulfill them unconditionally.[1] In other words, the idea of covenant is simply a divine special providence expressed in religious language. One can even posit from a theological standpoint that the entire history of Israel itself is a marker for divine special providence.[2]

---

[1] For more detailed information about covenant in the Old Testament, see W. J. Dumbrell, *Covenant & Creation: An Old Testament Covenantal Theology* (Devon: Paternoster Press, 1984), 15-20.

[2] Cf. W. Pannenberg, *Offenbarung als Geschichte* (Göttingen: Vandenhoeck & Ruprecht, 1961).

[3] Cf. John D. Barrow, *Theory of Everything,* 12; Ian G. Barbour, *Issues in Science and Religion,* 44-55; A. N. Whitehead, *Science and the Modern World: Lowell Lectures,* 18.

[4] Lynn White, Jr., "The Historical Roots of Our Ecological Crisis," in *Science* 155 (March 10, 1967), 1203-7.

[5] For more about the Priestly motif of the first account and the Yahwist motif of the second account see Hans Schwarz, *Creation,* 169-172.

The Priestly creation account in Genesis is, without a doubt, the first text to which one must turn in order to discuss a biblical understanding of creation. The fact that its mythic formula is incompatible with modern cosmology is by no means grounds for denying its importance, particularly when it comes to ecology. Even hardened scientists offer testimony to Genesis' relevance, both as to its epistemological impact on modern science[3] and to the close connection between the Creation Story and the progression of ecological deterioration.[4] In light of the historical context of the account's composition, the underlying motif is primarily the theological[5] acclaim of God as the highest, supreme Lord over creation. The text therefore downplays the importance of celestial bodies and spiritual powers worshipped by other contemporary peoples living side by side with Israel. But though the motif is primarily theological, the providential character of creation has never lost its focus. One of the discernible pieces of providence in the account is the divine dictation of necessary natural conditions (e.g.., "Let there be light."). The creation of sun, moon, and other celestial bodies; the separation of land and water from each other; the positioning of the heavenly vault to retain water vapor (an ancient understanding of atmosphere), the cultivation of trees, plants, and grass: all can be interpreted as preparation for the physical conditions necessary for life. Given the scientific development at the time, the biblical worldview is actually rather sophisticated compared with those offered by other ancient religious traditions.[6]

It is a deplorable fact that the Priestly creation account is normally construed as a divine warrant to subdue and exploit nature without limit.[7] Nature is seen as an object for the gratification of physical need, a simple matrix possessing absolutely no intrinsic value of its own. Its value and

[6] Wolfhart Pannenberg believes the account in Genesis to be in line with scientific views and explanations of the origin and development of life. See W. Pannenberg, *Systematic Theology* vol. 2, trans. Geoffrey Bromiley (Grand Rapids: William B. Eerdmans, 1994), 116-130.

[7] Rosemary Radford Ruether, *Gaia & God: An Ecofeminist Theology of Earth Healing* (New York: HarperCollins Publishers, 1992), 19-22.

[8] Salai Hla Aung, *The Doctrine of Creation in the Theology of Barth, Moltmann and Pannenberg*, 42; also see Karl Barth, *Church Dogmatics* III.1, 97.

[9] Cf. H. Paul Santmire, *Creation and Nature: A Study of the Doctrine of Nature with Special Attention to Barth's Doctrine of Creation* (Th.D. Dissertation: Harvard University, 1966).

merit are usually measured in terms of the degree of its availability for human exploitation. The model paves the way for human beings to conquer and control nature according to their will, and it is by no means foreign to the modern mind. Even the writings of renowned theologian Karl Barth reflect this rubric, evident in the formulations Barth develops for his understanding of creation. Barth understands "covenant as the inner basis of creation and creation as the outer basis of covenant."[8] The underlying idea is ostensibly simple: covenant, i.e., God's election of humanity in Jesus Christ before the time of creation, is the inner basis of creation. It is the ground as well as the reason for God to realize creation materially. The flipside of Barth's coin, creation as the outer basis of covenant, defines creation as the setting for the unfolding events of salvation history. What logically follows is the idea that creation exists for no purpose other than to make itself available for the practical performance of God's covenant drama with humanity.[9]

The two versions of the creation story in the Bible provide no direct warrant for human beings to treat nature with contempt, especially the Yahwistic Genesis 2 account: "Out of the ground the Lord God formed every beast of the field and every bird of the air, and brought them to Adam to see what he would call them. And whatever Adam called each living creature; that was its name" (2:19). The tone and the flow of thought in this text convey the motif that the other creatures are companions for the human being. Indeed, one can interpret the naming of the creatures as the God-bestowed bond between the human and animal kingdoms. The kind of exploitative language that characterizes Genesis 1 ("subdue the earth and have dominion over all the living creatures") is totally absent in the second chapter. In light of 2:9, "and out of the ground the Lord God made every tree grow that is pleasant to the sight and good for food", the "companion" paradigm becomes apparent. God offers grains, cereals, and fruits as the staple foods of human beings. Animals, by contrast, are originally intended to be sources of joy and friendship rather than of nourishment.[10]

Even the first account respects the idea that the animals are companions

---

[10] It is in the covenant with Noah that other creatures are referred to as food (Gen. 9:3). This inclusion of other creatures as food can be seen as a consequence of the Fall, Cf. R. R. Ruether, *Gaia & God*, 65.

and helpers for human beings. The command in verse 28, "subdue the earth and have dominion over all the living creatures", has a completely different connotation in the context of verse 29: "And God said, 'See, I have given you every herb that yields seed which is on the face of all the earth, and every tree whose fruit yields seed; to you it shall be for food." Accordingly, the command "to have dominion over all the living creatures" by no means implies a warrant for exploiting animals as food. "Have dominion over them" could refer instead to the taming and domesticating of animals for specific tasks like tilling the soil, carrying burdens, drawing carts, riding, etc.

Even more important is the twofold character of the command. Myopic anthropocentrism typically accounts for an over-emphasis of the "subdue and subject" decree at the expense of the moral obligation. If these two sides of the command are to receive equal attention, the result could be a dominion over animals by taming and domesticating them while at the same time proactively caring for their wellbeing. This point becomes clear if we consider it in light of Gen. 2:15: "Then the Lord God took the man and put him in the Garden of Eden to tend and keep it." Here the text clearly underscores the moral obligation: the human being is created and entrusted to the task of being a caretaker for the environment, so that it will continue to fulfill its divine intention of being productive and good, in and of itself. If the stewardship of nature stressed in Gen. 2:15 receives the same consideration as the "dominion" command of Gen. 1:28, one has a proper theological foundation for the human supervision of the ecosystem. Instead of being the decisive source for human exploitation of nature, an accusation often leveled upon them, the Genesis accounts admonish human beings to be conscientious in relating with the surrounding environment. Had such a balanced interpretation been the accepted model all along, perhaps the current environmental situation would have been altogether different.

The Genesis accounts would have offered insight into the very root of

---

[11] Cf. Sallie McFague, *Models of God: Theology for an Ecological, Nuclear Age* (London: SCM Press, 1987), 9.

[12] Cf. *Ibid.*, 12.

ecological balance if the depth of their testimony had been grasped in earlier eras. Gen. 2:7 reports that the human being is created out of earth. This association with the soil reveals the intimate bond between human beings and nature, especially the radical dependency of human beings on the earth in every stage of their life cycle. In the spirit of feminist theology, one could argue that nature indirectly gives birth to humanity.[11] Nature is the source not only of birth, but also of human prosperity; by contrast, nature requires no form of human contribution for its welfare.[12] Human existence would come to a sudden end if nature did not exist, while nature would suffer nothing if the reverse were true. The reality is that, though human beings have received everything that they have through the God-given medium of nature, they have offered staggeringly little in return. This physical and sensory image of the human being molded from clay soil has been ignored or even downgraded in favor of the spiritual, amorphous image of God breathing life into the human being.[13] As with the moral obligation of ecological stewardship, the physical and earthy representation of human origins has been sorely missed. In its absence, a lofty spiritual lopsidedness emphasized the subjective aspect of human existence, and nature was doomed to objectification and exploitation.[14]

Although the unity of mind and body, of spirit and matter, has been upheld and underscored in Jewish thought, only the spiritual side of life came to be emphasized in the Christian tradition. This one-sided emphasis on the subjective aspect of life was initially spawned and further fortified by the negative perception of matter in ancient philosophy. In ancient Greek philosophy, matter, i.e., the physical aspect of life, was considered deficient and profane. It was mortal, and thus it was evil.[15] Being evil in its very

---

[13] Cf. R. R. Ruether, *Gaia & God*, 29f.

[14] Cf. *Ibid.*, 30.

[15] Here we can point to the teachings of Gnosticism and Manichaeism as examples. The negative perception of flesh can also be observed in the teaching of Paul: Rom. 7:5; 8:5-8: Gal. 5:17; 19-21; 24: Eph. 2:3.

[16] For instance, in Paul and John (1 Jn. 2:15-17).

[17] This type of salvation teaching is usually found among charismatic and fundamentalist Christian groups, cf. *Evangelical Dictionary of Theology*, ed., Elwell, 205-205, 433-435.

essence, matter (nature) should be treated with the utmost contempt. It logically follows that matter is the cause of all problems and malice in human existence. By subjugating matter humans can overcome the forces of evil and save themselves spiritually. Some features of this sort of dualism can even be found in the Bible.[16] Directly or indirectly, this distortion further gave rise to the development of the doctrine of salvation strictly in terms of otherworldliness. Christians are not to strive for gain in this world but must aim their efforts to life beyond. Salvation is not attainable in this world, because this world is nothing but evil matter. It is imbued with all sorts of temptations, a breeding ground for any kind of worldly vice imaginable. An Exodus-type soteriology, i.e., salvation in terms of forsaking the world in search of spiritual "pie-in-the-sky", is the result.[17] This sort of salvation teaching is popular and attractive to the common mindset. The world takes on an "Egypt" quality of slavery: a realm of evil powers and a home of destitution, despair, and suffering. There must be an Exodus – the world must be forsaken, the believers marching forward with total trust in the protection and guidance of God through the wilderness into the promised land of the next spiritual world. This sort of distorted soteriology teaching only helps foster a negative perception of the world and contempt for nature.

The mode of soteriology which is both theologically apt and ecologically helpful is an incarnation-type salvation. When one keeps Christ's incarnation in focus, the world is no longer a forsaken realm of bondage but a domain with a God-given destiny. It is no evil and heinous place to be shunned, but the very good creation of God. One is expected to follow in the footsteps of the incarnate Christ by entering into the world and working to transform it into the Kingdom of God. This conversion occurs by establishing love, peace, justice, equality, and righteousness not only among human beings but also between human beings and nature. God's will is thereby fulfilled here on earth. When it comes to salvation,

---

[18] For more about the religious festivals in Jewish culture, see Rabbi David Kirshenbaum, *Feast Days & Fast Days: Judaism Seen through Its Festivals* (New York: Bloch Publishing Company, 1968).

[19] Cf. *The New King James Version* (Nashville: Thomas Nelson Publishers, 1990), 146f.

therefore, the physical and the spiritual are not easily divided. An incarnation-based soteriology embraces the salvation of the whole person, which includes that person's relationships in the human and ecological communities. This model is more in line with the biblical teachings about what "salvation" truly means. God's tangible promise to the Israelite people that the land of Canaan will flow with milk and honey; the incarnation of Christ in human form to establish God's kingdom here on earth: both attest to the fact that God wants His people to be physically saved while they are still living here in this world. Nature no longer needs to be shunned and forsaken but loved and cultivated so that it accomplishes its destiny to be a blessed home for all human beings.

God's salvific providence is also prominent in the Jewish tradition of religious festivals.[18] There are seven major religious festivals in Judaism:[19]

1. The Feast of Passover and Unleavened Bread. This is one of the three pilgrimage feasts, and it is held in commemoration of God's deliverance of Israel out of slavery in Egypt. The main features of the feast include the slaughtering and consumption of an unblemished one-year-old male sheep or goat on the day of Passover (Ex. 12:5, 48), the eating of unleavened bread for the following seven days (Ex. 12:15:20; Lev. 23:6), the observance of the first and seventh day of this week-long period as "holy convocations" (Lev. 23:7-8), the offering of special sacrifices (Lev. 23:8; Num. 28:19-24), and the presentation of the first fruits to the priests (Lev. 23:10-14).

2. The Feast of Pentecost. Another of the three pilgrimage feasts, Pentecost is also known as First Fruits, Harvest and Weeks. The underlying idea is to give thanks and praise to God for his abundant providence in nature through the fecundity of the land and the abundance of rain that provide for a bountiful harvest in the field. Special offerings were presented in the temple in biblical times (Lev. 23:17-20).

3. The feast of Acclamation or Trumpets. This is a festive religious celebration commemorating the arrival of the New Year. This celebration is a reminder of God's goodness and steadfastness in adhering to his covenant promises by guiding the regular progression of seasons and years.

4. The Day of Atonement. This is a holy convocation on which all the Jewish people, both priests and people, are to humble themselves before God and pray for his forgiveness (Lev. 16, 23:27-32; Num.29:7-11).

5. The Feast of Tabernacles. The last of the three pilgrimage feasts, it lasts for seven days and is also called the Feast of Booths, Ingathering, or Succoth. It commemorates God's accompaniment, protection, and guidance through the wilderness wanderings, as well as his gift of a good harvest. The people are to live in booths made of tree branches to represent the way they lived in the wilderness (Lev. 23:40,42). Special offerings of thanksgiving were presented in the temple to commemorate the harvest (Lev. 23:37-38).

6. The feast of Hanukkah. This is the Festival of Lights or re-dedication of the temple in Jerusalem. It is a joyful celebration that lasts for a week and a day.[20]

7. The feast of Purim. It commemorates God's protection of the Israelite people through Esther from the plot of Haman in Persia. It is celebrated in the reveling spirit of eating, drinking and giving gifts.

Five out of the seven feasts result from the Israelite people's understanding of God's providence. The festivals of Passover and Unleavened Bread, Purim, and Tabernacles are concerned with thanksgiving offerings to God for his special providence in the historical life of the Jewish people. The festivals of First Fruits, Acclamation, and Tabernacles likewise remember and commemorate God's general providence in and through nature. Through the celebration of these festivals, the Jewish people recall the

---

[20] On each of the eight days, a new candle is kindled and added to the previous ones in order to reflect the miracle associated with the festival's origin. It is reported that when the Hasmoneans defeated the Greeks and took control of the temple in Jerusalem, they searched the entire premises for oil to kindle the menorah. They could find only one small container of oil, enough to burn only a single day. But a miracle occurred, and the oil burned for eight days consecutively. See Rabbi D. Kirshenbaum, *Feast Days and Fast Days*, 118.

[21] For more information see Per Larsson, *Your Will Be Done on Earth* (Hong Kong: Clear-Cut Publishing & Printing Co., 2004), 87-90.

constant presence of divine providence, a reminder that keeps the relationship between Israel and their God alive and strong. A sense of thanksgiving remains alive in their lives, and this has helped to arouse the awareness of their obligation toward animals and nature. The keeping of the Sabbath tradition in Old Testament era is entirely consistent with this moral consciousness. Unlike the ritual observances of its Jewish origins, Christian culture in general lacks a proper tradition of thanksgiving for God's providence. Per Larsson is correct in his assessment that Christians should develop a culture of thanksgiving for God's activity in nature in its liturgical observances.[21] If such a culture of thanksgiving were developed and widely practiced, it would resurrect an awareness of the Christian's vital obligation toward nature and other creatures. It would serve to remind the church constantly of God's loving care in and through nature, which would in turn foster a spirit of gratitude and respect for the natural order. The United States of America is an example thereof: among "Christian" nations, the United States is noteworthy in keeping the culture of thanksgiving to God for his providence. This reminds the people constantly about the love and care of God in the history of their nation. Of course, this is probably one of the reasons why religious consciousness is still alive and well in the US, compared to the traditional Christian nations in Europe.[22]

There are many possible methods to develop the culture of thanksgiving in the Christian community's worship life. Churches can hold special sing-song services periodically throughout the year, services featuring hymns composed and written specifically to reflect the wonder and nearness of God in nature. Some of the songs should aim at demonstrating the overarching beauty of nature, whereas others should draw attention to the continuous fecundity of the land, the cycle of seasonal change, the sufficient downpour of rain, and the benefits of good weather. Churches can also hold periodically special drama programs with the intention to illustrate the nurturing purpose of the ecosystem, the ecological realities in our environment, the pain and cry of the whole creation, etc. If films showing the special functions of nature, the fine-tuning of the world, and the concrete cases of nature's deterioration were displayed at

---

[22] Cf. Kenneth Scott Latourette, *A History of Christianity*, vol. 2 (San Francisco: HarperSanFrancisco, 1975), 1253-1274.

such programs, it would be quite helpful in arousing public awareness of ecological problems. As the old adage goes, "a picture is worth a thousand words," and a film concerning ecological issues could effect spiritual and ecological benefits. Churches could also focus their Sunday School programs on scriptural texts that describe the bountiful providence of God in nature, and pastors could glean their sermons from the texts of these passages. These measures would aid churches in developing a "green" theology to provide assistance in the struggle against the ecological crisis. They would help tremendously in restoring a true rapprochement between human beings and nature. In so doing, they would also contribute significantly to the spiritual growth of the believers.

Allusions to God's providence within nature are evident in the religious Sabbath traditions in the Old Testament times. The concept of the Sabbath is an outstanding source of ecological values. The Sabbath in its three biblical forms – Sabbath day, Sabbath year, and Jubilee – are a significant theological formulation of a conservation ethic. Jürgen Moltmann could not be more correct in describing the Sabbath as God's conservation strategy.[23] But the problem with the Old Testament Sabbath tradition is its one-sided emphasis on religious observance. It overlooks and forgets the conservation commitment. In other words, Sabbath as God's protective measure for human and ecological wellbeing is absent. It is simply a religious obligation to be strictly observed and enforced. It is precisely this static Sabbath context that pits Jesus and the Pharisees against each other in the gospels. Whereas the Pharisees emphasized strict religious observance, Jesus stressed a seamless blend of worship and conservation-minded action. His heightening of the Sabbath's protective purpose is manifest in his declaration: "The Sabbath was made for man, and not man for the Sabbath" (Mk. 2:27). To interpret the Sabbath along ecological lines implies a day for rest not only for human beings but also for the whole of creation. In that way they could renew and resuscitate themselves from a day of rest on the Sabbath.

---

[23] Jürgen Moltmann, "The Ecological Crisis: Peace with Nature," in *The Scottish Journal of Religious Studies* 9 (1986), 12f.

[24] The following are the requirements of the Jubilee: the granting of respite to the land Lev. 25:11, 12, 18-22; the restoration of property to the original owner Lev. 25:23-28; for restoration of liberty to the enslaved Lev. 25:38-43; for remitting of debt to the debtor Lev. 25:47-55.

This idea of renewal through Sabbath rest resounds in the Leviticus descriptions of the years of Sabbath and Jubilee. The Jewish people are enjoined to let their fields remain fallow every seventh year and in the year of Jubilee.[24] One could argue for an inherent ecological implication here, even though such language is not used, per se. The land would be allowed a year to recuperate from the burden of the previous six, and animals would benefit by grazing on unplowed pastureland. Interestingly enough, the Jubilee provisions also require the landholder to return his property to the original owner; the underlying idea is that the land belongs to God, who alone has a legitimate claim to it. If interpreted the other way round, the children of Israel are living on borrowed land, and the theological implication of providence is clear. Possession of land is not a status symbol, a reason to be proud, if one doesn't own it in the first place. With the demand to change ownership comes the indirect admonition to treat the land and all of its benefits with respect, something of intrinsic value that precludes exploitation. Israel can cultivate the land, but it must do so with great care. The extra-human creation is thus granted divine protection from unbridled human exploitation.

It would, of course, be fundamentally impossible for the Christian community to apply such practices to its Sabbath traditions. Nevertheless, there is substantial room for Christianity to learn from the ecological implications of the Old Testament Sabbath and Jubilee traditions. Both are excellent signs of God's provision of land and the ensuing human responsibility for the conservation of natural resources. The unfortunate ignorance of these symbols in the Christian tradition gave rise to the inclination to subordinate nature to human desire. Christian culture has failed to instill in most people a sense of respect and gratitude for natural resources. A spirit of negligence and exploitation is the fruit of this failure. The Old Testament practices cited above can broaden the Christian understanding of God's concern for physical wellbeing, thereby altering the majority's attitude toward an acceptance of nature's intrinsic value. And Jesus of Nazareth, with his emphasis on the community of people and with his healing miracles, is thoroughly coherent with conservation.

5.2   God's Providence in Nature in Jesus' Teaching

As is the case with the Old Testament records, the gospel accounts of Christ's teachings contain definite allusions to divine providence. Jesus points to both special and general providence in his miracles, sermons, and parables. He does so in spite of the knowledge that the Jewish people are already well informed of providence through the Law and the Prophets. Jesus' providential framework is peculiar from a Jewish perspective: rather than being centered solely upon what God has done in history, it focuses on His future promises and sees providence through new eyes. This fresh spiritual insight of this shift is of profound theological significance. The specific gospel texts that include Jesus' hermeneutic of God's providence are as follows:

1. Mt. 5:45: "God makes his sun rise on the evil and on the good, and sends rain on the just and on the unjust," cf. Lk. 6:35.

2. Mt. 6:26: "Look at the birds of the air, for they neither sow nor reap nor gather into barns; yet your heavenly Father feeds them," cf. Lk. 12:24.

3. Mt. 6:28-29: "So why do you worry about clothing? Consider the lilies of the field, how they grow; they neither toil nor spin; and yet I say to you that even Solomon in all his glory was not arrayed like one of these," cf. Lk. 12:27.

4. Mt. 10:29: "Are not two sparrows sold for a copper coin? And not one of them falls to the ground apart from your Father's will," cf. Lk. 12:6.

5. Mt. 10:30: "But the very hairs of your head are all numbered," cf. Lk. 12:7.

One of the underlying theological motifs in Jesus' providential hermeneutic is to remind his audience about God as Creator and his Lordship over the whole of creation; this is especially the case in Mt. 5:45.[25] Besides his emphasis on the justice of God in letting his sun shine and rain fall on all alike, Jesus might also have wanted to illustrate that God's grace is readily

---

[25] Here one should take into account Jesus' definite choice of the genitive pronoun "his" instead of an article "the" with respect to the main objective of his statement, i. e., the sun.

[26] Here one recalls the ancient worldview: the earth as understood as a wide, flat land, and the sun, moon, and stars reigned in the sky. Cf. Wolfhart Pannenberg, *Systematic Theology*, vol. 2, trans. Geofrey Bromiley (Grand Rapids: William B. Eerdmans, 1994), 116-119; see also Rabbi D. Kirshenbaum, *Feast Days and Fast Days*, 17. The use of the rainbow as a sign of God's covenant with Noah is reflective of this ancient cosmological understanding. Technically speaking, rainbow and clouds are directly related to sun and rain.

observable in such ordinary phenomena as sunshine and thunderstorms. Sun and rain are the most important factors for the prosperity of life. They are also two of the foremost features of ancient cosmology, even virtually identical with the cosmos itself.[26] If one applies Adolf von Harnack's methodological caveat to approach any given text in its original cultural framework and paradigm, then Jesus' reference to sun and rain could be a direct indicator of God's benevolent activity on the cosmic level as well as his daily preservation of physical wellbeing. Jesus thus reminds his followers of the divine foundation upon which their life is ontologically dependent.

Moreover, by referring to the sun and rain, Jesus reminds the people of the indiscriminate love and care of God for their lives. The regularity of sunrise and rainstorm is an appropriate natural symbol of God's steadfast love according to the ancient worldview (Cf. Jer. 10:12-13; Gen. 1:16-18; Ps. 89:36). Jesus wants to convey (and does, in so many words) that God is a good shepherd who always cares for the security of his flock. The way God loves the world reveals him to be entirely trust- and praiseworthy. God is the moral paragon, encouraging people to struggle for justice with full confidence in the source of all justice, his righteousness. God admonishes them to remember that he is the source of all good things, of all true enjoyment. Failure to acknowledge this is tantamount to a denial of God's existence, for any earthly blessing is a sign of divine benevolence. Theologically speaking, the denial of God's existence is the beginning of our estrangement from God, and accordingly it is also the beginning of our estrangement from the natural order, God's created sphere for human life. One should therefore never fail to return thanks to God for the congenial environment he provides.

Mt. 6:26 is another allusion to God's providence. Jesus offers the illustration of the birds of the air, which "neither sow nor reap nor gather into barn," to point out that God is the one single source of all physical needs for both humans and animals. At face value it would appear that Jesus' choice of this image is not especially extraordinary, derived as it is from something that people see virtually every day. But if one delves deeper into the concept and explores its implications for life, then there is the profound possibility for grasping the true character of life. The intended meaning appears quite obvious: God takes care of the birds by feeding them with grains and fruits, whether the plants grow wild or through human agriculture. And yet, this naïve explanation is probably not what Jesus meant to convey. What the text implies is the very truth encoded in the mystery of life itself: God is the force who causes those plants to germinate and grow. Indeed, God is the font of all sustenance, the author and owner of life. Unless God as life-force fashions the seed, there will be no grass, vegetables, plants, or trees of any kind, and animals and human beings will go without food. The metaphysical reality behind the "bird" illustration is that God is the foundation on which the survival and continuation of life depends. Paul expounds on the hermeneutic in 1 Cor. 3:6-7: "I planted, Apollos watered, but God gave the increase. So then neither he who plants is anything, nor he who waters, but God who gives the increase." It is both utterly logical and infinitely wondrous; and yet humanity habitually fails to notice or take seriously the fundamental root of life. The gospel accounts and the letters of Paul both portray life as a precious and fragile gift of God to be respected and revered.

This depiction of life as precious gift is gradually taking the form of scientific fact. Again: all scientific efforts to produce a single living cell have failed, despite painstaking care to determine the proper ratios, components, and conditions.[27] This failure all but proves life to be a God-given legacy, a divine bequest beyond duplication or price. The utter sanctity of life is implicit in the text and is perhaps the true force behind Jesus' choice of words.

Yet another example of Jesus' providence hermeneutic (and another bird allegory, to boot) is Mt. 10:29: "The falling of the sparrow to the ground does not occur without the will of God." The force of the passage lies with the falling of the sparrow. The sparrow's demise is simply an event, one that God controls like any other natural occurrence. When one recognizes the myriads of sparrows that fall (and are born) daily, the logical implication is that God controls every natural event in the world. The Hebrew understanding of natural event clarifies the issue: God, according to the Jewish mindset, is the driving force behind every change in nature. This insight has shaped the Jewish understanding of history, particularly the history of Israel and its development. God is with His people throughout

---

[27] For more, review the discussion in chapter 3.

[28] Cf. Rabbi D. Kirshenbaum, *Feast Days and Fast Days*, 19-22.

their history. He is behind and within history, driving it ever onward. Historical events are thus the direct result of God's actions, and He controls the unfolding of history through His personal engagement in the world process. Put simply, He is Lord over history. Because the developmental course of the world has been directed by God through His participation in it, history is moving toward higher and higher levels of progress. The course of historical development is thus linear and irreversible.[28]

By offering the image of the falling sparrow, Jesus brings into focus the Jewish belief of God's unilateral lordship. Jesus reassures his audience that their history and destiny, both as a people and as individuals, rest in the hands of God. Their life experience is not the product of happenstance but the direct result of divinely-determined purpose. If they are happy with their lives, then they should thank the author of their story. If they are dissatisfied, then they ought to examine introspectively their commitment to God. For God, the overall Lord of history, is also intimately imbedded in the immediate social setting where individual stories find themselves being unfolded and molded. And yet despite God's certain control, human participation and contribution in the process should never be questioned. When life situations move from bad to worse, the blame should not be placed upon God; rather, this deterioration results from the failure of the people. They have no appreciation for the work of God in their lives, and therefore there is no positive response on their part. In short, human sin lashes out against divine providence with apathy and self-centered smugness in the arena of history.[29] Christians should therefore always place the question of gratitude at the forefront of their stories: "Do I have an appreciation for what God has done in my life?" and "Is my own contribution in stewardship and conservation consistent with my obligation?"

Jesus' statement in Mt. 10:30 is rather intriguing, using as an example God's numbering of the hairs on one's head. This case in point is a clear indication of God's special providence. Count all the hairs on a human head would be a convoluted and complex task. And Jesus uses this example to point out precisely this intricacy and perplexity. Methodologically speaking, one can argue that Jesus is speaking indirectly of God as the

---

[29] Prophetic messages are a good proof of this.

origin of all the laws of nature, the One who sets them in motion and continues to control their operation. Hair grows and falls out because of the biochemical processes of the body. This kind of special providence is not foreign to Jesus' disciples, who were raised in the tradition that everything proceeds according to God's will through the processes he has established. Ps. 139:13 is a prime of example thereof: "For you have formed my inward parts; you have woven me in my mother's womb." So too is Psalm 148, which underscores God as Creator of all things, visible and invisible, who keeps them in order by his decree (a religious term for the law of nature) that shall not pass away (cf. 148:5-6). When taken together, Mt. 10:29 and Mt. 10:30 reveal that Jesus wants to encourage his followers in the face of possible persecution and ensure them that the Lord who is above all worldly powers and authorities is fully in control.

Speaking within the context of scriptural tradition, Jesus points to the lordship of God over all the physical laws of nature and the dependability of their continuous functioning. All natural phenomena, including hair growth (and loss), progress according to God's marvelous providence. To review briefly, chapter 2 described how modern science has revealed the natural systems of earth's ecosphere – as well as the natural order in the solar system – to be incredibly fine-tuned, and that this fine-tuning has made possible the emergence and prosperity of life on this earth. The human obligation to participate in the ecological story, to keep it balanced and operating as God intended it, is truly consistent with a life lived in thanksgiving.

In Mt. 6:28-29 Jesus says: "So why do you worry about clothing? Consider the lilies of the field, how they grow; they neither toil nor spin, and yet I say to you that even Solomon in all his glory was not arrayed like one of these." The apparent allusion to God's providence notwithstanding, there is a more important lesson to be gleaned, an admonition to obey. The comparison between the flowers of the field and the royal splendor of Solomon gives one pause; if Jesus wanted to point only to simple providence (i.e., God looks after the lilies), then the comparison would be entirely unnecessary. Relating the lilies to Solomon's majesty means he wants his disciples to consider the comparison itself. Solomon, one recalls, is recognized as the wisest king in the history of Israel, the expanse of his kingdom the largest, his material treasury the greatest. Jesus therefore emphasizes that divine providence in common things – like flowers – far surpasses the royal grandeur of the richest, wisest, and ablest monarch that ever reigned in Jerusalem. In this way he cautions his followers to humble themselves before God and not to take pride in earthly achievement. Human achievement is never comparable to the innovation of God's work in creation. As demonstrated in earlier chapters, modern science has uncovered countless natural novelties and wonders. These discoveries, whether subatomic or galactic in scope, show the raw wonder of God's design, and soundly resonate with Jesus' lily allusion. The following are but some of the myriad examples of the novelty and wonders of Creation.

Scientists from industrial nations are working together to produce enormous volumes of energy by emulating the nuclear fusion inside the sun. A pilot project to construct a reactor using this fusion technology is planned to occur in France in the near future. The estimated cost for this attempt is no less than 10 billion Euros, and the lifespan of the project is estimated to run about 35 years.[30] That end results of the venture are, at this stage, purely speculative. Even if the attempt is successful and the technology produces sufficient power, the practical costs of placing it on the market will be staggeringly high. Such difficulty makes one appreciate all the more the abundant free energy God provides through solar fusion, the supply of which is guaranteed for another several billion years. To talk about energy should therefore bring special providence automatically into perspective, and with it a corresponding gratitude.

The successful design and manufacturing of rockets that can travel at the speed of more than 10,000 miles per hour is a good reason to take pride in human ingenuity. Rockets make life more enjoyable – without them, for instance, there would be no such thing as satellite television. The launching of rockets has transformed the world so significantly that it has become a "small village", especially with respect to communication technology. Satellite telecommunication networks offer the ability to speak

---

[30] Cf. Manfred Dworschak, "Sonnenofen in der Provence," in *Der Spiegel*, Nr. 20 (May 14, 2005), 165.

[31] Norman Myers, *The Gaia Atlas of Future Worlds: Challenge and Opportunity in an Age of Change* (London: Gaia Books Ltd., 1990), 80.

immediately to anyone anywhere on the globe, not to mention seeing each other on the screen of the cellular phone.[31] Powerful rockets that travel great distances and at high speeds make this discourse possible. And yet: the breakneck speed of the rockets is negligible compared orbital speed of the earth. To recap, the earth orbits the sun at 66,600 miles per hour and produces a centrifugal force that keeps its orbital path stable. This is one of the natural factors that are crucial for the existence of life. Whenever we step on a high-speed airplane, we ought to remember this providential gift of planetary velocity and say a prayer of thanksgiving.

One of the most astonishing achievements in postmodern science is its success in the field of biology. Since the discovery of DNA in the 1950s, the progress of scientific research in biology has been incredible, both as to subject matter and to outcome. Biological breakthroughs have brought about many revolutionary developments such as cloning, genetically altered plants, genetic therapeutics, stem cell research, and biotechnological research. Although these breakthroughs are certainly incredible, they could not have been possible without using living organisms and cells as starting points. However innovative they may be in technological terms, they are of negligible import alongside God's creation of life from inanimate and unorganized material, whether directly or through the mechanism of evolution.

An exorbitant amount of money is required to send satellites into space for the purposes of networking and communication. Postmodern technology has enabled humankind to invent and apply a remote-guided or -controlled system for navigation and transportation through orbital communication-networking. Of course, this technology offers many social and economic benefits; but their price is considerable. God, on the other hand, has provided an infinitely more complex communication network through purely natural mechanisms – i.e., the earth's magnetic field. In point of review, the earth's molten core creates the magnetic field, thereby making possible the use of the compass for navigation.[32] All who sail the seas or traverse remote mountain ranges should take this providential act to heart.

---

[32] Cf. Gary A. Glatzmaier and Peter Olson,"Probing the Geodynamo," in *Scientific American*, vol. 292, No. 4 (April 2005), 33.

Many nations are spending several billion dollars each year for national security. To a certain extent, this expense brings about the desired result. On the whole, however, even this vast sum of money fails to provide a real and robust refuge from danger. Those who intend to harm a nation can still infiltrate its territory through gaps and inadequacies in the security network. And those security measures are aimed only at the small-time efforts of enemies on this planet. By contrast, to review once again, God has provided fail-safe extraterrestrial protection from meteors and solar winds. Merely stepping outside and taking a breath of fresh air should therefore be adequate grounds for shouting thanksgiving to the God who maintains such solid security.

The huge dams and hydroelectric power plants that have sprung up and spotted the landscape are also signs of postmodern scientific progress. Indeed, economic benefits from the construction of dams are huge, for they facilitate large annual agricultural harvests. A population is thereby able to produce more than enough food for human consumption and for industrial capital. Hunger and starvation are easily avoidable, and the fields of many nations "flow with milk and honey" because of this technology. Hydroelectric plants, too, provide an invaluable service: electricity at a minimal price, both to communities and to industry. And once again, these human efforts are trifling beside the immensity of the world's oceans, a God-given natural reservoir. It is indeed ironic that something so vast could be overlooked and taken for granted. The benefits the seas provide – discussed in detail in chapter 1 – remain a remarkable example of ecological providence.

The invention of the computer is too unique to escape notice. Like all past innovations in mechanized production (e.g., the assembly line), computerized systems have radically changed the way people live, work, and think. Computerization aids the emergence and acceleration of globalization, an economic phenomenon that draws people in different lands closer together while simultaneously driving communities apart. It draws people together in worldwide business, but it drives away local job opportunities. Computer proficiency has become the professional pulse of life. Those who know how to use this tool can make their way in the

---

[33] Cf. Kwabena Boahen, "Neuromorphic Microchips," in *Scientific American*, vol. 292, No. 5 (May 2005), 39.

world and become financially successful; those who do not are simply left out of the race. There are therefore multiple positive and negative features of postmodern computer technology. Computers are certainly awe-inspiring; but once again, they are overwhelmingly primitive compared to the sheer complexity of the organic computer, i.e., the human brain. One almost never remembers to give thanks to God for this highly complicated organic computer, created and placed safely within the natural protective cover of the skull.[33]

Jesus' spiritual admonition to subordinate the majesty of kingly accomplishment to the simple complexity of wildflowers reminds the human race to avoid the pitfall of achievement arrogance. The far superior work of God is readily observable, both within one's own life story and in the beauty of natural surroundings. The story of Solomon himself adds credence to this rebuke; because he takes such great pride in his personal success and fails to see it a blessing from God, he estranges himself from God, thus paving the way for his kingdom's downfall. Solomon is in this sense an archetype of sinful selfishness, for everyone falls victim to the deification of personal success. Self-absorption leads one away from God, who is in reality the sole author of all the conditions necessary for us to enjoy prosperity. To be estranged from God is to fall away from the foundation of life, sinking into a downward spirally, socially, and ecologically. In light of Christ's admonition, we ought always remind ourselves of the greater and superior work of God in nature and give him thanks and praise in all things. This life-orientation of thanksgiving will help to heal the broken triune relationship between God, human beings, and the natural order. The next section will delve into the Pauline metaphor of one body with many parts. Much more than a mere ecclesiastical illustration, it is a holistic symbol that offers new insight into the concrete ecological reality.

5.3 One Body with Many Parts and Its Ecological Implications (Paul)

In his first letter to the church at Corinth, St. Paul speaks of all believers belonging to the Body of Christ, i.e., the Church: "For as the body is one

---

[34] Paul was brought up in Tarsus, which was at the time an economically successful and prosperous city. It had all kinds of schools of rhetoric. Cf. Jerome Murphy-O'Connor, *Paul: A Critical Life* (Oxford: Oxford University Press, 1997), 33-35.

and has many members, but all the members of that one body, being many, are one body, so also is Christ" (1 Cor. 12:12). He continues the illustration in verse 26: "And if one member suffers, all the members suffer with it; or if one member is honored, all the members rejoice with it." Paul is attempting to remind the congregation that they are one in Christ by pointing out the easily recognizable interdependence of all the parts of the human body. Exactly how Paul came to use this physical analogy to express the relationship between Christ and the Church is an intriguing question, indeed.

Given the cultural context of the church in Corinth, Paul could have gleaned this analogy from Greek philosophical works, most of which was well known to the people.[34] In the tradition of Stoicism, for example, the world is construed as a living being similar to the modern Gaia construct.[35] The relationship of human beings to this organic world and to each other is that of a part to a whole: the world is a macrocosm, a colossal living being, and the human beings as microcosms therein. They are linked to each other, bound closely together by the *logos*, the rational principle indwelling in everything.[36] God and the world are identical, and the relation between them resembles something of a soul/body distinction. The world is the visible body of the invisible God, and God is the invisible soul of the visible world. The logical inference from this philosophical outlook is that all living things are parts of this greater world-being, whereas the world-being is an organic colossus embracing all others into her essence. This world-body needs all the micro-beings, and vice versa. They are mutually related and thus live the same life together. If one small part suffers, all the others (including the world-being) also suffer. If one micro-being rejoices, all the others also rejoice, for they dance to the same rhythm of life and continue in the constant

---

[35] The prevailing philosophical fashion in Tarsus at the time of Paul was said to be Stoicism, Cf. C. K. Barrett, *Paul*, 8. Some even think that Seneca, the main Stoic exponent in the Roman Stoa, maintained close correspondence with Paul. There is further speculation that Paul was responsible for Seneca's conversion to Christianity; many, however, are doubtful of this speculation. Cf. Marcia L. Colish, *The Stoic Tradition from Antiquity to the Early Middle Ages* (Leiden, The Netherlands: E. J. Brill, 1985), 16.

[36] Cf. Marcia L. Colish, *Ibid.*, 22-27.

communion of the indwelling *logos*.

The similarity in tone and substance between the Stoic cosmology and Paul's body metaphor is unmistakable. Their difference resides in the way they understand the relationship that binds the parts to the whole. In Paul's view the relational character of body to the parts is compositional. Parts are simply the constitutive components of the body; the relation between them is *direct*. According to Stoicism, by contrast, the relational character is structural. The parts are not constitutive components of the whole; they are related to the whole structurally. The relationship between them is thus *indirect*. In spite of this significant distinction, however, the two views are analogous in that the parts and the whole are interrelated and interdependent. Both the similarity and dissimilarity demonstrate that Paul was well acquainted with the school of Stoicism.[37] It is probable that he took this Stoic idea and adapted it to suit his purpose. Whatever the case may be, one thing is certain: both Paul's "Body" illustration and the Stoic "World-being" cosmology can serve as conceptual tools to visualize what the ecosystem is and how it works. The way the ecosystem is composed and functions greatly resembles a body with many interdependent parts and systems. If follows the model presented by the Stoic worldview or the Gaia hypothesis, the picture becomes one in which the world is a great Mother and everything else her offspring. Mother and children relate to each other in a mutually beneficial way through the genetic bond of the ecosystem. When the Mother suffers, the children suffer also. When the Mother rejoices, the offspring also rejoice, because they share life from the same ecological fount. The ecosystem is thus the linchpin in the web of life. As noted earlier, the continuation of life depends directly on the smooth functioning of the ecosystem, just as the ecosystem depends directly upon the healthy operation of the organisms within. Both are mutually dependent and

---

[37] Paul's upbringing in Tarsus, his teaching about God's general revelation in Rom. 1:20f, and his invocation of the unknown God in Acts 17:22f all hint that he was well acquainted with ancient Greek's philosophy.

[38] Cf. Sallie McFague, *The Body of God: An Ecological Theology* (Minneapolis: Fortress Press, 1993), 8-10.

[39] Cf. Wesley Granberg-Michaelson, *Redeeming the Creation. The Rio Earth Summit: Challenges for the Churches* (Geneva: WCC Publications, 1992), 12, 16.

mutually benefiting. Life will deteriorate without the support of the ecosystem, and the ecosystem will collapse without the balance of constituent systems and lives.

The atmosphere, the ocean, life activities of organisms, inland water systems, continental divides, the political territories of nations, regulative natural mechanism: all are integral parts to the ecological body. The most meaningful characteristic of this relationship is its high degree of interrelatedness and interdependence.[38] What happens to one happens to all; when one lacks something (or is absent altogether), the others feel the deficiency.[39] Each system is fundamentally vital, not only for the body's structural health of the body but also for its smooth functioning. The following examples provide concrete evidence of this ecological interdependence.

The phenomenon of global warming and its attendant climatic anomalies are prime examples of a deficiency in environmental interrelatedness with respect to both cause and effect. As indicated earlier, the primary cause of global warming is the increased human emission of greenhouse gases. The sources of these emissions vary geographically and consist mostly of a few industrialized and overpopulated countries. These gases do not remain stationary in the sky above those nations, of course, but dissipate around the planet through atmospheric flows.[40] The result is that comparatively innocent nations feel the full impact of global warming. The consequences can be horrible, including a variety of natural disasters in almost every part of the world. Again: the problem caused by some of parts affects the whole in its entirety. Global warming has caused the melting of glaciers capping the top of high mountain ranges and icebergs in the polar regions. The consequences of this thaw will be widespread: severe floods will occur in rivers fed by glaciers. The level of

---

[40] Cf. Wesley Granberg-Michaelson, *Redeeming the Creation*, 74f.

[41] See the pictorial illustration by Norman Myers in his *The Gaia Atlas of Future Worlds*, 72f, 89, 91, 93, 99, 103, 105.

[42] Cf. Craig Simons,"Beware of Falling Ice," in *Newsweek* (June 6/ June 13, 2005), 83f.

[43] Cf. *The Gaia Peace Atlas: Survival into the Third Millennium*, ed., Frank Barnaby (London: Gaia Books, 1988), 211; also Norman Myers *The Gaia Atlas of Future Worlds*, 140.

the seas will rise, submerging coastal cities and towns worldwide.[41] If all glaciers were to melt away completely, as they may very well do in a couple of centuries,[42] many of the world's largest rivers, ecological lifelines, will be without a water supply and dry up. Along with this gradual drought, the natural habitats of many wild animals – and some groups of human beings – will disappear from the surface of the earth. These ominous predictions underscore just how important the earth's ecological interdependence really is.

The world's forests also provide ample testimony to ecological interdependence. The forests are the lungs of the earth's ecosystem:[43] like their organ counterparts, the forests help sustain and regulate the life and working of nature's ecosystem through the twofold activity of photosynthesis and transpiration. The awarding of the Nobel Peace Prize to a tree-planting ecologist in 2004 clearly reflects the significance of forests for ecological health. The Amazon forest in Brazil regulates the regional ecosystem in American continents, and the Equatorial forest in central Africa maintains the ecosystem on that continent. Those monsoon forests of Asia perform the same function in the orient. All together, these forests inject life-energy into the ecosystem and act as earth's circulatory system. But they are recklessly reduced year after year by commercial logging companies, and this deforestation is progressing faster than ever before. The ongoing depletion of the rain forests in Africa will invite drought into the continent, eventually converting the whole of the continent into desert.[44] And the same could very well happen in America and Asia if their respective rain forests are destroyed.[45] What one part of the ecosystem suffers causes larger problems in other areas. How hard is the human heart, how egoistic is human ambition, that civilization refuses to pause from its endless exploitation and adopt a sense of appreciation for nature's efforts? The presence of forests and their contribution to ecological wholeness thus

---

[44] Regarding the link between deforestation and drought and other ecological problems, see Frank Barnaby, *The Gaia Peace Atlas*, 211.

[45] Cf. Norman Myers, *The Gaia Atlas of Future Worlds*, 77, 89, 94, 95.

[46] For more information see Janet N. Abramovitz, "Imperiled Waters, Impoverished Future: The Decline of Freshwater Ecosystems," in *Worldwatch Paper* No. 128 (Washington, D. C.: Worldwatch Institute, 1996), 11-30.

demonstrate – and when it comes to human thoughtlessness, tragically so – how interdependent the planet's systems really are.

As hinted above, the interrelatedness within the ecosystem can also be found in the circulation of water across the world. From an ecological point of view, oceans, lakes, ponds, rivers, and streams collectively make up the lifeblood of the environment. There is in fact a strong metaphorical resemblance to the human circulatory system: oceans and lakes are like the four chambers of the heart, rivers are the major arteries and veins, and smaller tributaries and streams are the capillaries branched across the body. Like the human circulatory system, this natural system is highly interconnected, resulting in an entirely undisturbed flow of water. Any damage done to any part of the system will damage the distributive function of the whole. Damming of a big river or restructuring a river system is like cutting off one of the major arteries in the human body.[46] Without a preliminary study of the surrounding area and a well-planned preventive scheme for dealing with any possible problems, damming a river will effect considerable environmental damage.[47] There is continuing criticism and strong opposition to the huge dam development in China called Three Gorges Project. The project's immediate ecological consequences are the destruction of wild animal habitats and the relocation of people.[48] How it will affect the underground water in the region and impact the area's climate remains to be seen.

The diverting of water from rivers and streams for purposes of irrigation and industrial use is another example of cutting the blood vessels of nature's life.[49] Diversion of water implies a blockage of blood flow into the life of a region. This deficiency in turn disturbs the area's equilibrium

---

[47] For more information see Sandra Postel, "Dividing the Waters: Food Security, Ecosystem Health, and the New Politics of Scarcity," in *Worldwatch Paper* No. 132 (Washington, D. C.: Worldwatch Institute, 1996), 26-35.

[48] anet N. Abramovitz, "Imperiled Waters, Impoverished Future," 22f.

[49] Cf. Sandra Postel, "Dividing the Waters," 29-34.

[50] Cf. Norman Myers, *The Gaia Atlas of Future Worlds*, 95; also Sandra Postel, "Dividing the Waters," 32-34.

[51] Sandra Postel, "Dividing the Waters," 29f.

and eventually leads to the regional ecosystem's total collapse. This exact problem is currently happening in the region around the Aral Sea. The Sea's water level has declined rapidly in recent years because of unchecked irrigation, and the result is the emergence of vast areas of salt desert and severe climatic changes.[50] The same situation is true of the Ganges River and its basin in India, and the Nile and its basin in Egypt.[51] These crises demonstrate that ecological balance bears a striking resemblance to Paul's "Body" analogy. Just as the destruction of a small part in the human body like a small blood vessel can lead to the death of – or cause severe pain to – the whole body, the industrial damaging of various parts of the ecosystem like water diversion or deforestation can lead to the eventual suffering and death of nature itself. Seemingly small and insignificant elements are crucial to nature's wellbeing; one would do well to remember this truth and to the pitfalls of untamed egoistic ambition.

The apostle Paul continues his "Body" analogy in 1 Cor. 12:21-22: "And the eye cannot say to the hand, 'I have no need of you;' nor again the head to the feet, 'I have no need of you.' No, much rather, those members of the body which seem to be weaker are necessary." Our consideration of nature's ecosystem shows that every part is equally important and necessary for the survival and health of the whole. For instance, a human being cannot say to the tiny organisms in the soil, "we do not need you because you are too small and cannot speak our language," just as it is thoughtless if an American says to the Kuwaiti people, "we do not need you because your country is so small and does not have the kind of political system we value and practice." Those tiny organisms in the soil are in fact the invisible factories that manufacture natural fertilizers for the fecundity of the soil. And yet, how much harm has been done to those tiny creatures, humanity's most beneficial life partners, through the use of industrial toxic insecticide, artificial chemicals, and careless waste dumping? How much damage have they suffered from merciless human arrogance? They cry for help with the whole of nature, calling for mercy in a language both inaudible and incomprehensible to human beings. But their cry is totally intelligible to God, their Creator and Caretaker.

The following prayer relates something of the cry of those tiny organisms and the contribution they provide to the earth through their life and labor.

God, we thank you for the small creatures that decompose our wastes,

the blind workers beneath us in the soil,

the bacteria, the worms, the fungi and the insects,

the diligent workers making new fertile soil,

those who we trample under foot.

Spirit of life, you know their silent language,

confer our thanks to them. Greet them from us human beings

who live just a short while here above the earth.

Tell them that we are dependent on your work and also that

we together with you are family, since even we humans come

from the ground and will once again return to the dust.

Greet them and tell them that we are glad

for the fruits of your endeavors every day.

May God bless you, small brothers and sisters in the compost,

members of the congregation beneath the soil.

May you keep your health and appetite forever! Amen[52]

God, the Spirit of life, joins the cry of these tiny workers to the painful groaning of the entire Creation as it longs for liberation. This Pauline image and its ecological relevance will comprise the focus in the next section.

5.4   The Groaning of the Creation and Its Liberation

In Rom. 8:19 Paul states that "the creation waits in eager expectation for the sons of God to be revealed." In verse 22 he continues, "We know that

---

[52] This prayer is formulated by the Lutheran Church in Sweden and is cited by Per Larsson in his *Your Will Be Done on Earth*, 43.

[53] The religious training Paul received at the feet of Gamaliel is important in view of the fact that Gamaliel was not an ordinary teacher. He was an informed and learned mentor whose theological knowledge and intellectual wisdom earned him a reputation of great respect among his people. See Jerome Murphy-O'Connor, *Paul*, 55f.

the whole creation has been groaning as in the pains of childbirth right up to the present time." If one takes this text at face value, it seems rather prophetic, for it appears to predict the modern ecological crisis. But if one places the text against the backdrop of Paul's theological training, it becomes clear that Paul is not foretelling a future ecological disaster so much as addressing the ecological problems of his own time. His ecological perspective is more theological in meaning; however, this does not mean that it has no direct implications for the present ecological crisis. Rather, Paul provides a story that will help modern eyes the ecological crisis in a more spiritual light.

To better understand what Paul says in the text, one must first consider the importance of his theological background. Scripture informs that Paul was trained to become a theologian in Judaism (Acts 22:3; Phil. 3:5).[53] Having studied Jewish theology and tradition, Paul was more than likely well acquainted even with the more esoteric thoughts related to Jewish doctrine. Among these esoteric traditions was the kabbalistic tradition,[54] an attempt to develop a holistic or panentheistic view of the world with the Spirit of God as a unifying ground.[55] In other words, it is a theological construct in which the whole creation finds itself upheld and nurtured by the protection and care of God's Spirit.[56] From a literary point of view, one can see a similar theological concept in Col. 1:16-17: "All things were created by him and for him. He is before all things, and in him all things hold together."

If one approaches the kabbalistic doctrine of holism in conjunction

---

[54] Cf. *The Kabbalah Unveiled,* trans. S. L. MacGregor Mathers (London: Arkana, 1991), 1-6. Kabbalism was originally passed down from generation to generation orally, especially among the trained clergy. Cf. *ibid.,* 5f. Here one can note the importance of Gamaliel's emphasis that Jewish religious tradition was kept in two forms, namely written and oral. Cf. Jerome Murphy-O'Connor, *Paul,* 56.

[55] Cf. Mathers, *Ibid.,* 25.

[56] To a certain extent, the way the world is pictured and explained in kabbalistic doctrine bears resemblance to that of Stoicism. For more about kabbalistic doctrine, see Mathers, *Ibid.*

[57] For the meaning of the terms *ruach* in the Old Testament and its conceptual implications for creation, see Jürgen Moltmann, *The Spirit of Life: A Universal Affirmation,* trans. Margaret Kohl (London: SCM Press, 1992), 40-43.

with the Jewish understanding of the term *ruach*, the result is the Spirit of God upholding and nurturing the whole of creation by dwelling within it all times and in all places.[57] This indwelling Spirit of God gives life to everything in creation and holds them together with its ubiquitous presence. The underlying idea is similar to what the Psalmist says in Ps. 139:7-10: "Where can I go from your Spirit? Where can I flee from your presence? If I go up to the heavens, you are there; if I make my bed in the depths, you are there. If I rise on the wings of the dawn, if I settle on the far side of the sea, even there your hand will guide me, your right hand will hold me fast." Ps.104: 29-30 is another such testimony: "When you hide your face, they are terrified; when you take away their breath, they die and return to the dust. When you send your Spirit, they are created, and you renew the face of the earth." Everything is alive and safe because they are kept in the life-giving power of the indwelling Spirit of God. God's Spirit is thus the source of life, the unifying foundation of all things, and everything is upheld within it. If one assumes that Paul combines the teaching of kabbalism with the Genesis creation accounts and subsequently arrives at the formulation of whole creation groaning in pain, the picture becomes a web of Spirit in which everything finds and occupies its respective place, undisturbed yet unified.[58] The lion rests together with the calf, while the tiger plays together with the deer. The relationship between creatures is so amicable that they build up together a peaceful and harmonious community. Like these other creatures, human beings also find their place in this universal peaceful community. As for food, they no longer need to till the soil or to kill other beings. They live by eating the food that is supplied naturally. There is therefore no enmity, no fighting, and killing among the creatures; so there is no pain, groaning,

---

[58] It is difficult to say exactly where Paul took the idea of the groaning of the whole creation in pain. Cf. Olle Christoffersson, *The Earnest Expectation of the Creature: The Flood-Tradition as Matrix of Romans 8:18-27* (Stockholm: Almqvist & Wiksell International, 1990), 39-45. Taking into consideration Paul's teaching of one body with many parts, one can argue that he might have learned about the kabbalistic doctrine from Gamaliel. He could have then mingled it with the Jewish understanding of the terms *ruach*, Jewish apocalyptic teachings, and the creation story in Genesis to constructing his own concept of the groaning of the created order in pain.

or suffering due to competition, oppression, or exploitation. All creatures share life peacefully under the care of the indwelling Spirit of God. Creation is in a perfect state of peace and harmony, the obvious outcome of the nurturing care of the indwelling Spirit of God. This situation is precisely the beautiful and harmonious picture of life in the Garden of Eden before the fall. Eden is the essence of peace and harmony: the human beings live together with other creatures and do not need to toil the ground for food. They enjoy life by taking what nature provides. There is no enmity between humans and other creatures. Everything is perfectly ordered in Eden: harmony rules supreme.

Theologically speaking, this beautiful harmony and order in the Garden has been turned upside down by the Fall. Post-lapsarian life resembles quite the opposite of the Garden's prevailing pattern: enmity, competition, fighting, bullying, killing, oppression, and exploitation became the order of the day. Creatures become enemies of each other and fought and killed for survival. A species of one kind must live in fear of another, and thus it tries to keep as far away as possible from the encroaching threat. The order of life is no longer a harmonious drama but a battle in which the clever and the powerful always gain advantage over the weak and naive. The peaceful relationship that exists between the creatures and their surrounding environment is also affected by the Fall, becoming strained and broken. Human beings, considered the crown of creation, have to toil the ground and kill other creatures, their immediate neighbors, for food. Both creatures and nature become the object of humanity's merciless oppression and exploitation in order to gratify its physical needs. The powerless have to suffer constantly the injustices and oppression of the mighty. Even among the stronger, there is always an internal fight for superiority and survival. No one is free from fear, and all equally receive and undergo the painful attacks of others in one way or another. The whole creation is, indeed, under the reign of sin and injustice: it is groaning and crying in pain. Even the indwelling Spirit of God feels this intense suffering, and it groans and cries together with the whole creation (Rom. 8:26). Figuratively speaking, the original paradise is lost. In its place reigns a notorious and life-threatening darkness. The original world characterized by peace, beauty, harmony and order becomes a veritable hell on earth. Creation thus trembles with anticipation, waiting for the liberation from the enslaving reign of this alienation.

Theologically speaking, the sole objective of the incarnation is the redemption of this broken relationship between Creator and creature, as well as between the creatures and their surrounding environment; in other words, to restore the lost paradise of Eden. Christ becoming a human being restores the broken covenant and sets a new covenant in its place. This purpose is discernible in the words of Jesus at the Last Supper: "This cup is the new covenant in my blood, which is shed for you" (Lk. 22:20). The death of the Son on the cross accomplishes the atonement of sin, i.e., the alienation of the broken covenant. Christ's death is meant to bring the whole creation back to being at-one with itself and with its Creator. An important factor in this respect is that God's covenant never intended human beings alone to be covenant partners, but the covenant includes all other creatures and nature as a whole. God's original covenant with Adam and then with Noah both offer authority to this interpretation. In the former, the bringing of animals to the human being and the command to tend and keep the Garden imply the inclusion of other creatures and nature in the covenant. In the latter, God's command to Noah to take on board pairs of animals and the divine cleansing of the earth's surface with the floodwaters reveal that other creatures and the environment are also included in the covenant.

The idea of "covenant" is a mutually beneficial relationship. The old covenant that was established with the original creation was broken at the Fall, and thus was no longer the rule of life. The consequence was, as discussed above, the loss of paradise and the emergence of darkness and suffering. It was to this fallen creation that the Son of God came. He did so in order to redeem, restore, and bring back the world to its original life, a life of complete harmony. The question is whether this objective of the Son's mission has been achieved or not. It is rather tempting to provide a hasty answer to the question; in any case, one can say that Christ achieved the mission partially but not completely. The reconciliation of human beings with God the Father through the life, death, and resurrection of Jesus Christ can be described as a partial achievement of the Son's mission in the world. But when it comes to the question of the reconciliation between human

---

[59] Cf. Sallie McFague, *The Body of God*, 116f.

[60] Cf. *Ibid.*, 118-129.

beings and between human beings and the natural order, then the answer is apparently negative. Fully 2000 years after the death and resurrection of Jesus Christ, we human beings still live under the illusion of actual life and find ourselves at odds with each other socially, economically, and politically.[59] When it comes to the human relationship with other creatures and ecology, things become even uglier and more disheartening.[60] Other creatures and nature suffer still at the injustices and oppression of humanity. They are still groaning and crying in pain that human beings have inflicted upon them through merciless oppression and exploitation. The mission of the Son to restore the broken covenant for the whole of creation is still far from being fully realized. Ongoing action for the restoration of the broken covenant is still a challenge for the Church and the community. At this point all believers should bear in mind the earnest expectation of the whole creation for liberation from human abuse. Christians carry an uncompromising duty to carry on the redeeming work of the Lord.[61] By fulfilling this duty in the context of covenant restoration, one performs a holy service for God's Creation.

> Paul's teaching about the groaning of creation in pain and anticipation of liberation shows that right relationship is crucial for the flourishing of true peace in the whole of creation. Likewise, the essentially relational quality of modern Trinitarian reflection provides further insight into the ecological question.

5.5 Relational Trinitarian Thought

There is a new emphasis on the idea of relationship by Trinitarian thinking in modern theology. Though the origin of this new emphasis had nothing to do with ecological concerns, its methodology provides an excellent means for addressing the ecological crisis. It would be helpful to consider briefly some of the traditional views of Trinitarian thinking in order to better understand relational Trinitarian thought and to learn how various Trinitarian doctrines affect the environmental question. The traditional Trinitarian positions to be considered here are the *modalistic* view and the

---

[61] The challenges and programs raised and discussed in the book *Redeeming the Creation* issued by WCC are good examples in this respect.

[62] For more information regarding the modalistic and monarchical views, see Jürgen Moltmann, *The Trinity and the Kingdom of God: The Doctrine of God*, trans. Margaret Kohl (London: SCM Press 1981), 129-48.

monarchical view.[62] These two views are theoretically different in substance but are principally the same in essence. Both positions try to achieve the legitimacy of the monadic God or the endorsement of the monarchy of the one God.

In the modalistic view, the nature of God is considered in terms of substance. Because the three persons of the trinity are seen to have a common divine substance, they are viewed as one and the same person. The "differentiation" among the three persons is simply a variety of modes for the manifestation of the one God. The appearance of the one God in the form of three persons is seen only in connection with the idea of the creation of the world and the work of redemption. Regarding the inner being of God's self, the logical necessity of the three persons disappears, as the three persons are considered to be three-in-one in substance. God is thus only to be conceived in Trinitarian terms where His creative and redemptive work is concerned and not with respect to His being.

> In the monarchical view the nature of God is viewed in terms of a single subject. God is the One Subject who acts according to His will. The different persons of the Trinity are simply different modes of the One Subject's being, and activities of the three persons are simply the repeated act of the One Subject. What logically follows is the transfer of action to an unknown deity concealed behind the three persons. Like the modalistic view, the monarchical view places no stock in the necessity of social relationship between three persons in the inner life of God.

> Considering God along these lines will probably lead one to a narrow understanding of the true nature of God. This distortion will eventually result in the deterioration of human relationships. Jürgen Moltmann holds the modalistic and monarchical views of God directly responsible for the deterioration in the relationship between human beings and between human beings and their surrounding nature. He believes that these two views encourage individuals to look self-centeredly upon themselves in relation to others or nature.[63] The consequences resulting from this kind of outlook is a distortion in the relationship between human beings and between human beings and

---

[63] Cf. Salai Hla Aung, *The Doctrine of Creation in the Theology of Barth, Moltmann and Pannenberg,* 106f.

[64] See Salai Hla Aung, *Ibid.*

nature, or the oppression and exploitation of one another and of nature.[64]

The relational concept of the trinity, however, takes an entirely different approach from the two views discussed above. It stresses the importance of relationship instead of putting emphasis upon the unity of divine will or substance. Central to the relational concept of the Trinity is its assumption that relationship is the basic principle of everything. That is to say, relationship is basic to everything if everything is to continue in its present form and state. Already explicit in this assumption is that relationship is the most fundamental principle of life. There will be no life without relationship, or vice versa. The two are inseparably related to each other. Therefore, for God to be a living God, there must be a relationship. In order for a relationship to be present, there must be an existence of more than one being. What follows is a syllogistic deduction that God is Trinitarian from the very beginning. And it is precisely because of the relationship of the three persons of the Triune God that He is a living God and continues to be so. This logic indicates that there must be a separate and independent existence of the three persons.[65] Only when the three persons exist separately and independently can they enter into a personal relationship with each other. And this relationship is the fundamental assumption of the relational concept of Trinity.[66]

Crucial to this assumption is the notion that relationship is a nurturing ground for the circulation of life. In other words, life begins in and with relationship and continues only when that relationship goes on. Seen in

---

[65] Here the question of the "origin" of the Trinity would need to be explained. In this respect, I agree with Moltmann's view. That is, God the Father is seen as the origin of the three persons with regard to their hypostasy. The originality of God the Father is, however, valid only for the emergence or begetting of the Son and the Holy Spirit, not for their deity. For more see Moltmann, *The Trinity and the Kingdom of God*, 177.

[66] For more see Moltmann, *The Trinity and the Kingdom of God*; Wolfhart Pannenberg, *Systematic Theology*, vol. 1, trans. Geofrey Bromiley (Grand Rapids: William B. Eerdmans, 1991), and also his "Father, Son, Spirit: Problems of a Trinitarian Doctrine of God," in *Dialog* 26 (1987), 250-7.

[67] The relational concept of the Trinity, on the other hand, tends to convey the idea of tritheism, as it emphasizes separate and independent existence of the three persons. My suggestion for this shortcoming is that the three persons are

this perspective, the relationship within the triune God is the foundation of the circulation of life within the inner being of God, and the continuous relationship of the three persons ensures the continuation of divine life. Not to be neglected is the fact that in the relationship of the three persons of the triune God, none of them holds a monarchical status over the others. They are all equally responsible for the circulation of the divine life through their mutually beneficial and symbiotic discourse. This clearly demonstrates that the mutually beneficial and symbiotic relationship of the three persons is the eternal fount of the divine life within the inner being of God. Conversely, one can say that the purpose of this symbiotic relationship among the three persons is the circulation of divine life to ensure the continuation of divine being. And through their mutually beneficial relationship, a unity is upheld in the inner life of God. This unity in the inner life of the God is formed by the common desire of the three persons to support the wellbeing of the Trinity. This sort of unity must be considered to be an entirely beneficial relationship.[67]

Relational Trinitarian thought clearly shows that relationship and mutual reciprocity are the most vital and fundamental requirements for life if it is to continue and prosper. This project's consideration of nature's ecosystem thus far also indicates that relationship and mutual reciprocity are not only integral parts within the system itself but are also the very foundation upon which the continuation of the system is dependent. The question is whether one recognizes this fact and lives according to its logical requirements. Figuratively speaking, human beings, other creatures, and the overall environment are considered the most important parts of nature's ecosystem. Among these three, the human being is the most responsible for keeping nature's ecosystem healthy and working by entering into a mutually beneficial and symbiotic relationship with other creatures and nature. They may do so only when they recognize and accept the ontological truth that other creatures and nature do not exist simply for the sake of satisfying their physical needs but for the sake of ecological wholeness. Unless humanity recognizes the vital role other creatures and nature play in nature's ecosystem and the important contribution they make

---

of the same substance in such a way that they are indivisible and indistinguishable (Tertullian), while they are bound to each other too closely in terms of mode of being to make them distinguishable from each other.

towards its healthy continuation, they will never respect other creatures and nature as equal life partners. Moreover, ecology teaches that humanity has no right to claim superiority and proprietorship over them. Instead, human beings themselves are given life through nature and are thus subordinate to nature ontologically. By recognizing the vital contribution of other creatures and nature for ecological wholeness and entering into a mutually beneficial and symbiotic relationship with them, humanity enhances the chances of its own survival and future prosperity. The mutually beneficial and symbiotic relationship will also strengthen the very foundation upon which human life is dependent, and in this way human culture become richer and more beneficial than ever before. This discussion concerning the importance of relationship is in accordance with Christ's entreaty to love one's neighbor as one's self.

5.6   Jesus on the Good Neighbor

In light of all previous discussion, Christ's teaching about being a good neighbor becomes more and more relevant and challenging in spiritual, cultural, and ecological spheres. Technological advances have gradually – but radically – forged the earth into a global community. Easily observable marks of this global shift are the features that comprise the so-called information age: the internet, satellite and cellular communication, and world trade. Behind all these innovations lies the reality that the world has experienced and is still undergoing tremendous transformation in all aspects of life. Today the world is no longer as big or as vast as it was once thought to be. Instead, it has become a village – not only *in size*, but also *in nature*.

On the one hand, the world has become a village *in size* because the never-ending series of technological breakthroughs have diminished the distance and compressed the enormous space of the globe, reducing it (in accessibility) to the size of a basketball. On the other hand, the world is gradually becoming a global village *in nature*. Unlike societies of the past, populations the world over are becoming more and more colorful and heterogeneous in composition. Communities that were once totally homogeneous have now become veritable social mosaics. The former ethnic and language barriers distinguishing countries from one another have rapidly broken down. The social structure of today's world community is now being categorized as multicultural.

The process of economic globalization helps accelerate and intensify this process of social integration. Modern trans-national corporations redefine traditional boundaries and forge nations into a kind of borderless commercial empire. People are sent and regularly exchanged from one nation to another within this empire. The way modern globalization works and influences people is simply awe-inspiring; it would not be an exaggeration if we say that a development of this kind and at this scale is completely unprecedented in human history. Not even the vast political empires of the past can match this modern economic phenomenon. The medical cost of a patient in Europe and America can be immediately calculated and transacted electronically in Asia. Europeans and Americans work in factories that are owned and run by Asians, and vice versa. The globe is woven together into a kind of spider-web through the threads and strings of technologies and commercial ties. This process of globalization is both a blessing and a curse for the citizens of host countries as well as home countries. It is a blessing in host countries because it opens up new job opportunities for many people who would otherwise face unemployment.[68] It is a curse in home countries because jobs are sent abroad and given to others. The same is true with respect to how one reckons economic gain versus loss. Some believe that globalization allows the rich to profit at the expense of the poor. Others believe that both rich and poor will experience a gain; however, they believe that individual nations will experience a loss, their resources drained away into an international limbo. What is important, of course, is what matters most to the individuals concerned. After all, one thing is ever certain: the world is gradually being transformed into a global community of intercultural neighborhoods. There is no such thing as an "outsider" in this new socioeconomic reality, personal feelings or prejudice notwithstanding.

The nature of globalization is further accentuated and strengthened by the growing gravity of ecological problems worldwide. Just as there exists a close ecological interdependence on the global level, the same holds true in the economic sphere. The programs and policies that individual

---

[68] Cf. Daan E. H. de Roo van Alderwerelt, "Investment in Developing Countries: Privately-Financed Infrastructure, a Threat or an Opportunity for Development?" in *ICDA Journal: Focus on Trade and Development*, vol. 10, No. 1 (2000), 24-27.

nations have with regard to their respective economies have immediate consequences for all the neighboring nations on the global level. Denying the logical ramifications of either ecological or economic decisions is tantamount to a denial of the responsibility one has as a citizen and steward of the world. The closer the global community becomes both ecologically and economically, the greater the need for nations to take into consideration the wellbeing of their neighbors, as their own success and prosperity depends directly on that of their neighbors. Those who are unwilling to take seriously the ecological implications of what they do in their own territory allow themselves to be disqualified from the conscientious global community. These politicians and businessmen are rather like those robbers who fell upon the traveler on the way to Jericho. Though politicians across the world are trying to carve out spheres of economic influence for themselves, the ecological crisis and the necessity of global cooperation have brought the world's communities into a closer bond with each other. The growing globalization trend and the increased magnitude of the ecological crisis have a special socioeconomic, political, and ecological message to convey to everyone, both individually and collectively: human beings are no longer foreigners, strangers, and outsiders to each other. They are neighbors, friends, brothers, and sisters through the bonds of ecological interdependence and commercial globalization. Jesus' admonition to be a good neighbor is particularly relevant to this new global reality.

One finds in Christ's concept of the good neighbor the most profound aspect of religious teaching: morality and compassion toward the other. This principle is an integral and constitutive component for many of the world's religions. If one is to be true to the spiritual teachings of Christianity, one must be moral and humane towards the outer world. But a glance at the social relationships of people across the globe will reveal a different picture: the immoral and cruel treatment of people due to gender, cultural, and racial differences in both domestic and international settings. Worst of all, the immoral and inhumane behavior of human beings goes beyond its immediate social boundary and violates the ecological sphere. This is

---

[69] Cf. Wesley Granberg-Michaelson, *Redeeming the Creation*, 76f.

a clear indication that humanity is still far away from carrying out Jesus' call to be a good neighbor in one's daily life. This failure should summon all to radical self-examination and confession.

It is obvious that many of the social and ecological problems the world community faces today are entirely human-made. If one carefully traces the root cause of these problems, one will discover that they are characteristic of the immoral and inhuman behavior of fallen *Homo Sapiens*. The prevalence of human sin is reflected by the truth that though they know very well the profound implications of the present ecological crisis, they exhibit no change in attitude or behavior with respect to the environment. Though humanity often claims to understand nature as a gift of God, it still considers it a thing to be exploited without restraint. If a minor change of lifestyle means a big help in reducing the pain and suffering of the natural order, then one simply needs to make the change and be proactive. Using less energy, consuming fewer resources, and producing less waste is a start.[69] In light of the ever-growing increase in world population and its debilitating impact on the ecosystem, humanity ought to be willing to reconsider the theological and doctrinal position concerning birth control. Education on the importance of family planning for the upkeep of ecological and economic wellbeing will be a crucial step.[70]

Though all are well aware that nature provides a sheltering and nurturing environment, there is a striking hesitance to acknowledge that nature is similar to a human mother in this respect. Accordingly, the environment is due the same respect that one affords a human mother. If human beings had demonstrated an earlier willingness to consider nature as a living being with sensitivity and responsiveness, if they had shown a readiness to enter into a moral relationship with nature, then many of the current ecological problems would have been solved without recourse

---

[70] For more about the present trend of the world's population and its associated ecological problems, see Lester R. Brown, Gary Gardner and Brian Halweil, "Beyond Malthus: Sixteen Dimensions of the Population Problem," in *Worldwatch Paper* 143 (Washington, D. C.: Worldwatch Institute, 1998).

[71] Cf. R. R. Ruether, *Gaia & God*, 205-274.

[72] Cf. Leonardo Boff, *Ecology & Liberation: A New Paradigm* (Maryknoll, New York: Orbis Books, 1995), 52f.

to technology.[71] As it now stands, such a change in posture will help humankind in shaping ecological practices into better and higher forms, thereby returning the wounded natural order to its original state of harmony and beauty, a circumstance mirrored by life in the Garden of Eden before the Fall.

Here the life of Francis of Assisi, named the patron saint of ecology, is particularly helpful. The liberation theologian Leonardo Boff would say that there are two aspects of ecology in the life of Francis, an inner and outer ecology. Inner ecology is the deep appreciation for divine love and care in nature within one's own inner life. Outer ecology is being grateful, respectful, and kind in one's outward relationship with other creatures and nature as a whole for the many good things they contribute to the wonder of life.[72] To follow the life of Francis and walk in his steps is to follow Christ's admonition to be a good neighbor. This path will no doubt transform the world into a better habitat for all neighbors, human or otherwise.

CHAPTER 6

Concluding Observations

As regards the profuse natural sources for knowledge about God's providence in nature the Book of Job points out:

But now ask the beasts, and they will teach you;

And the birds of the air, and they will tell you;

Or speak to the earth, and it will teach you;

And the fish of the sea will explain to you.

Who among all these does not know

That the hand of the Lord has done this,

In whose hand is the life of every living thing,

And the breath of mankind?

Job 12:7-10

Just as Job has shown in the above text, what we have studied thus far in this work reveals God's providence in things we encounter in the world. Theologically speaking, things in the world directly or indirectly proclaim the existence of God and his goodness through the very nature of their existence and life. In the following we will summarize what we have discussed before, and also make some suggestion as to how we should go on further with the ecological realities in our life environment.

6.1   The World as the Best of All Possible Worlds

As mentioned above, Philosopher Leibniz had once asserted that "the world is the best of all possible worlds." Leibniz's assertion is not conceptually formulated, but is an empirically-based assertion of the worldly reality. It is empirical in that it takes its cue from the observed harmonious order in nature.[1] Compared to modern time the scientific development at Leibniz's time was not advanced either theoretically or

---

[1] Cf. Bertrand Russell, *The History of Western Philosophy*, 567-571.

[2] Leibniz was born in 1646 and died in 1716. Industrialization began sometime around the year 1750. The first telescope was invented by a Dutch spectacle-maker Johannes Lippershey in 1608 and the first practically applicable telescope that was constructed for the observation of the outer space was built by the Italian scientist Galileo Galilei in 1610, see M. W. Worthing, *God, Creation, and Contemporary Physics*, 11. The telescope was not so powerful enough to observe the space beyond our solar system. The observation of the space at a greater distance on a galatic level can be described as a noteworthy scientific development in the 20th century. Leibniz was, however, fortunate enough, for he had had at his disposal the foundational data and basic information about the solar system laid down by such scientists like Nicolaus Copernicus, Galileo Galilei and Johannes Kepler.

[3] P. C. W. Davies and J. Brown, *Superstring: A Theory of Everything*, 93.

technologically.[2] That means that scientific observations of natural phenomena were not extensive, let alone the observation of the outer space at galactic level. But with the rapid advancement of science after the Second World War scientific investigation of natural phenomena has been so tremendous that science has been able to penetrate and analyze things both in the outer reaches of the sky and in the subatomic realm in minute detail. More and more about the inner structure and character of the atom has been brought to light, and now scientists are investigating and theorizing even the smallest particles of the atom which is tentatively given the name "superstring," the dimension of which is considered to be just 10^{-33} centimeters.[3] This tremendous success in scientific analysis of worldly reality has brought to light more and more detailed information about the way things are. We have demonstrated the profound implications this new scientific information has had for religious faith.

In the field of space study and observation the same degree of advancement has been achieved. With the successful launch of satellites into space and the invention of powerful telescopes human beings are able to better observe and study the structure and nature of the universe. As discussed above, more and more galaxies are found one after another across the universe, and their numbers have steadily increased that they now count several hundred billions in all. Each galaxy in turn has several hundred billion stars with their surrounding planets. That means that there exist several hundred billion stars like the sun of our solar system. Mathematically speaking, along with the increased numbers of the stars and their surrounding planets the probability of the existence of planets with living creatures on it has also increased. It is no wonder that nowadays

---

[4] *The Hutchinson Concise Encyclopedia,* 721.

we find many scientific fictions in circulation, depicting strange and bizarre creatures from other planets. The intriguing thing is whether or not living creatures could really exist on other planets. The important thing that needs to be seriously considered in this respect is the kind of life we find on this earth. As mentioned already above, the form of life we find here is that of a hydrocarbon-based form of life. Being so, the most fundamental necessity for life is the fact that the environment must contain a sufficient supply of those hydrocarbon elements and at the same time should have effective natural mechanism to keep the natural regulatory system of those hydrocarbon elements going on smoothly. This is the most vital physical condition and requirement for life to emerge on any planet. Unless this condition and requirement are met, life as we know it here on this planet could never emerge. Let's take a look at the physical condition and property of other planets in our solar system:[4]

[5] Mark Alpert, "Strange New World: Piercing the Haze, Huygens Gets a View of Titan's Surface," in *Scientific American*, vol. 292, No. 4 (April, 2005), 11f.

[6] *Ibid.*, 11f.

Planet	Constituent	Atmosphere	Distance from sun (in millions of km)
Mercury	rocky, ferrous	-	5.8
Venus	rocky, ferrous	carbon dioxide	108
Earth	rocky, ferrous	nitrogen, oxygen	150
Mars	rocky	carbon dioxide	228
Jupiter	liquid hydrogen, helium	-	778
Saturn	hydrogen, helium	-	1427
Uranus	icy, hydrogen, helium	hydrogen, helium	2875
Neptune	icy, hydrogen, helium	hydrogen, helium	4496
Pluto	icy, rocky	methane	5900

The physical condition and property of other planets in our solar system are apparently not congenial for the hydrocarbon-based form of life because all of the other planets, as can be noted in the chart above, lack the necessary hydrocarbon elements in their ground-surface environments as well as in their atmospheres. Recent survey of Titan, the satellite moon of Mars, by the European Huygens Probe shows no sign of animated creatures living on it.[5] It is believed that Titan could hardly generate and sustain the hydrocarbon-based form of life because its ground-surface environment and atmosphere contain mainly nitrogen and methane gases.[6] One can, however, argue that there can be forms of life other than those that are hydrocarbon-based. The other forms could be methane-based or hydrogen-based or carbon dioxide-based, etc. To the best of medical knowledge

---

[7] Remember all the 57 natural factors Ross has enumerated in proof of the fine-tuning of the universe. For more see his "Astronomical Evidences for a Personal Transcendent God," 160-169.

available at present these other forms are hardly conceivable from a biochemical point of view. Even if there existed other life forms, that life would not be as pleasant, enjoyable and comfortable as the life we are enjoying here on this earth. For the enjoyment and comfort of life is closely related with the kind of food it needs for nutrition and the easy and abundant availability of its supply.

One thing to be remembered, on the other hand, is that in order for this hydrocarbon-based form of life to emerge on the earth there need to exist many conditions and also a coordinated networking of natural factors, which we discuss more specifically in chapters 1 and 2. We have also learnt that those particular natural phenomena found in nature are called the fine-tuning of the world. Natural conditions and coincidences necessary for the kind of fine-tuning we discussed above are numerous and extraordinary as well.[7] This actually places constraints on the probability of the hydrocarbon-based form of life emerging on other planets. Even if some of the conditions are in place but others are missing, that would still prevent life from emerging. The case here is that the degree of improbability increases in direct proportion to the number of those necessary conditions, coincidences, and circumstances. The greater the number of those necessary natural conditions and coincidences is, the lesser the probability of life's emergence on other planets is. Taking into consideration all those natural conditions, coincidences, circumstances, and fine-tuning we discuss above the probability of life's emergence on other planets is almost diminished. We can see more cogent explanation about this in the following argument of astrophysicist Hugh Ross:

> Let's look at how confining these limits can be. Among the least confining would be the inclination of a planet's orbit and the distribution of its continents. The limits for these are loose, eliminating only 20 percent of all candidates. More confining would be parameters such as the planet's rotation period and its albedo, which eliminate about 90 percent of all candidates from the contention. Most confining of all would be parameters such as the parent's star mass and the

---

8 *Ibid.*, 169.

9 *Ibid.*

10 Cf. Leonardo Boff, *Ecology & Liberation*, 15-18.

planet's distance from its parent star, which eliminate 99.9 percent of all candidates.[8]

He goes on to say:

> Of course, not all the listed parameters are strictly independent of the others. Dependency factors could reduce the degree of confinement. On the other hand, all these parameters must be kept within specific limits for the total time span needed to support life on a candidate planet. This increases the degree of confinement.[9]

We can note that in the above argument Ross has considered only few conditions, namely inclination of a planet's orbit and distribution of its continents, a planet's rotation period and albedo, the parent star's mass and a planet's distance from its parent star. Even on this basis 99.9 percent of the candidates are wiped out from the list. In view of all this, we can say with certainty that the probability of the emergence of hydrocarbon-based forms of life on other planets is almost unthinkable. That means that our planet earth is the best prepared dwelling place for us all. Science shows us that there exist almost countless other possible worlds in the universe, but our planet earth is the best of all these countless other possible worlds for the kind of life we are enjoying here on this earth. We read in the Bible that having completed the creation of the world God takes a look at the created world and says, "It was very good" (Genesis 1:31). In light of what we have discussed here, we would say that the planet earth is the most beautiful, pleasant and enjoyable place in the whole of the universe, and indeed is very good. The important thing is whether we are turning this best prepared dwelling place of ours into a bad place through our

---

[11] Cf. Janet N. Abramovitz, "The Imperiled Waters, Impoverished Future," 31-37.

[12] Cf. Christopher Flavin, "Rising Sun, Gathering Winds: Policies to Stabilize the Climate and Strengthen Economies," in *Worldwatch Paper* 138 (Washington, D. C.: Worldwatch Institute, 1997), 9-18; also Seth Dunn, "Reading the Weathervane: Climate Policy from Rio to Johannesburg," in *Worldwatch Paper* 160 (Washington, D. C.: Worldwatch Institute, 2002), 24-71.

[13] For more about Carl Gustav Jung's view see his *Modern Man in Search of a Soul*, trans. W. S. Dell and Cary F. Baynes (London: Routledge, 1997), 200-225.

careless and selfish way of life.[10] Let's consider this in the next section.

6.2 The Magnitude of the Challenge

The ecological crisis we face at present shows clearly the magnitude of the challenge ahead. It also reveals that the quality of our living space here on earth is steadily dwindling. The air we breathe for our life is no longer as clean as it used to be in the past. For the air in many big cities is now polluted by the emissions from industrial manufacturing activities and other life activities. The water we drink for the upkeep of our life activities is no longer as clean as it used to be in the past. Waters in lakes, rivers, and even in the underground wells are polluted with the wastes from industrial manufacturing activities and other life activities.[11] The climate that prepares a good living environment for the enjoyment of life by providing a congenial and productive weather is no longer as congenial and productive as it used to be. The atmospheric climate is perturbed with the increasing emission of greenhouse gases and aerosols from industrial manufacturing and other life activities.[12] Now is the time for all of us to reconsider the way we see, understand and treat nature. Unless we look back over the past retrospectively and learn things from those experiences in the past, the future would not be so promising for us both ecologically and socially.

Here we can see the importance of how the Swiss founder of analytic psychology, Carl Gustav Jung (1875-1961) viewed modern culture. The

---

[14] Some would argue that the present trend of global warming is part of natural cyclical process of climatic change. It is reported that climate undergoes regular alternation between ice age and warm period at the interval of every 10,000 years, and the next alternation is calculated to be entering into another turn of ice age. That means the earth is eventually going to be cooled down again despite the present growing trend of warming. Based on the statistical factors and scientific theoretical assumptions William Ruddiman has recently argued that the notion that the earth is eventually going to be cooled down again and enters into another turn of ice age is extremely impossible. For more see William F. Ruddiman, "How Did Humans First Alter Global Climate," in *Scientific American,* vol. 292, No. 3 (March 2005), 34-41.

[15] Janet N. Abramovitz, "Unnatural Disasters," in *Worldwatch Paper* 158 (Washington, D. C.: Worldwatch Institute, 2001), 8-37.

wrong which Jung sees in modern culture is our obsession with the present with our eyes fixed only on the future while totally forgetting the past.[13] But the important thing is whether human beings can go on this way into the future. The question is: Can we understand the present deeply enough without considering it in relation with the past which is the very fundamental necessity for the building up of a peaceful and prosperous society in the world? Most probably not since the present is the product of the past. In other words, we can symbolize the relation of past, present, and future in such a way that human cultures and human beings are born of the past and are being nurtured by the present while at the same time are being pulled forward by those goals set in the future. Figuratively, we could say that the present is bound to the past since it is tied to the past through the umbilical cord of time, and the past is inseparable from the present since it is the temporal womb in which the present finds itself being conceived and receives its lifeblood through the umbilical cord of historical continuum. Only when this temporal and cultural connection between the past and the present is well understood, and accordingly is always kept warm and fresh by the leaders of nations and societies across the world, will the future be healthy, strong, and fruitful for all of us and for the future generations of ours as well.

The problem is that many people as well as many nations seem unwilling to learn from the past especially with regard to the ecological problems we are facing at present. Numerous scientific observations and surveys clearly demonstrate that the global climate system is gradually changing for the worst. Over the decades the global temperature has steadily risen, and shows no sign of a sudden stop.[14] The upward trend of the global temperature's rise has been considered to be the prime cause

---

[16] Janet N. Abramovitz, "Unnatural Disasters," 8-14; also his "Infecting Ourselves: How Environmental and Social Disruptions Trigger Disease," in *Worldwatch Paper* 129 (Washington, D. C.: Worldwatch Institute, 1996), 31-52.

[17] Cf. Norman Myers, *The Gaia Atlas of Future Worlds*, 32f.

[18] *Ibid.*, 32f.

for the occurrence of many natural catastrophes causing great casualties both in terms of material belongings and human lives.[15] Nowadays the annual cost of material loss amounted to several hundred billion dollars while the human cost is of the same magnitude with several hundred thousand lives being sacrificed. Several powerful hurricanes slash US and Mexico one after another. Likewise, powerful typhoons (the Asian version of hurricane) visit and cause huge destruction in Japan, China, the Philippines, and several Caribbean nations. The occurrences of torrential floods worldwide are also numerous. There were torrential floods in China, Pakistan, Bangladesh, the United States, Brazil, etc. The total cost of these floods amounted to several hundred billion dollars. Many other emission-related natural catastrophes such as landslide, drought, and snow storms occur increasingly worldwide.[16]

On the other hand, what we need to do is to consider the question whether the ecological crisis we are facing today is surmountable or insurmountable. Given the technological and financial resources of the world we would say that the ecological crisis we face now is not insurmountable. The question is whether we are willing to combat it or not. For instance, it is scientifically observed that the main cause for the rise in global temperature is the greenhouse gas, viz., CO_2, from the burning of fossil fuels.[17] It is also observed that more than half of the total CO_2 being released into the atmosphere comes from this fossil burning.[18] It is evident that automobiles and power plants are the main source of the greenhouse gas emission. Given several hundred million cars running on

---

[19] For instance, the exact quantity of China coal production in 1996 was 1,397,000,000 metric tons, *2002 Britannica Book of the Year* (Chicago: Encyclopaedia Britannica, Inc., 2002), 580; the production of USA in 1994 was 937,580,000 metric tons, *ibid.*, 757; India's production for 1999 was 292,356,000 metric tons, *ibid.*, 631; and Russia's production in 1999 was 166,000,000 metric tons, *ibid.*, 711.

[20] Robert J. Samuelson, "The Dawn of a New Oil Era?" in *Newsweek* (April 4, 2005), 13.

[21] *Ibid.*

[22] Yvonne Baskin, *The Work of Nature*, 194.

[23] Paul Brown, "Melting Ice: The Threat to London's Future," in *Guardian Newspaper* (July 14, 2004).

the streets of all the nations across the world the huge addition of CO_2 gas into the atmosphere annually would pose no surprise to any one. The same is true with the many power plants across the world. Many power plants in the world including the United States rely heavily on coal as their main raw material. One can easily figure out how worst the situation would be from the consumption of coal even in a number of countries. It is reported that China alone extracts and consumes approximately 1300 million tons of coal per year. Almost the same quantity has been extracted and consumed in the United States. India, Russia and European countries, and other nations in the world are also extracting and consuming coal in huge quantity annually.[19] When it comes to the daily consumption of oil across the world, the picture is as bleak and alarming as that of coal consumption. It is reported that a total of 84 million barrels of oil is used up everyday.[20] It is calculated that if the present economic growth continues, then there will be some 150 million cars in China in near future.[21] The same story can emulate itself in another giant country, namely India. What will be the consequences ecologically when these two giants become the United States of America in Asia in terms of economic affluence? It is reported that even today several billion tons of CO_2 are released into the atmosphere annually.[22] Paul Brown, environmental correspondent, wrote in the Guardian Newspaper the following report about his interview with Dr. David King, scientific adviser to the British Prime Minister Tony Blair, in 2004.

> Records of the 3 km deep Antarctic ice core showed that during ice ages the CO_2 in the atmosphere was around 200 parts per million (ppm), and during warm periods reached around 270 ppm, before sinking back down again for another ice age. That pattern had been repeated many times in that period but had now been broken because of the intervention of men.
>
> CO_2 in the atmosphere had reached 360 ppm in the 1990s and now was up to 379 ppm and increasing at the rate of 3 ppm a year, reaching a level not seen for 55 million years when there was no ice on the planet because the atmosphere was too warm.
>
> I am sure that climate change is the biggest problem that civilization has had to face in 5000 years, he concluded.[23]

Dr. King described how the ice caps like those on Mount Kilimanjaro had been continuous for hundreds of thousands of years and survived through successive warm periods but are now expected to disappear in 30 to 40 years.

Dr. King warned of the slow response of the climate system and said we were already doomed to 30 to 40 years of climate heating because of the CO_2 already in the atmosphere, hence the need to multiply effective flood defense such as the Thames barrier.

Dr. King said because there was no ice on the planet 55 million years ago, it was impossible to tell how much CO_2 there was in the atmosphere but it was probable only slightly more than we are currently heading towards.

We have already pointed out that the world has had the technology to cope with this excessive emission of CO_2 by automobiles and power plants. The technology in the motor industry has made great advances in the last few years so that it can now manufacture cars with little emission of CO_2. Of course, the lifespan of such cars would be shorter compared to the ordinary cars, but it is not at an unaffordable cost given the affluence of people in modern time. The so-called hybrid car using a combination of combustion technology and fuel cell technology has been on sale. Biogas and ethanol cars which emit so little greenhouse gas are also now being manufactured. What needs to be done is to introduce a legal framework by government, which would encourage the production and use of such ecologically-efficient cars. What is more fascinating is that scientists had been successful in designing and producing a prototype engine using liquefied hydrogen. The technique works so miraculously that the engine emits no CO_2 at all. What it emits is only water vapors from the burning of the liquefied hydrogen in the engine's combustion chamber. The problem, however, is that this technology has not been applied practically to the benefit of all due to the lack of facilities for production and storage of the liquid hydrogen.

The same can be said about power plants. New technology which uses

---

[24] Dan Roberts, "Is Coal the Lowest Energy the World Is Looking for?" in *Financial Times* (August 17, 2004).

[25] This is what we will get if we calculate the cost in terms of the purchasing power parity of their respective national currency.

coal but emits no CO_2 at all is already available. Information about this new technology was reported in the *Financial Times* in 2004:

> The hunt for zero emission has also gone one step further through power plants that use a technology called gassification. In these plants, which have not yet been built on a large scale, coal is first converted into a synthetic gas before being burnt in a manner akin to the way turbines are used in natural gas power stations.
>
> In perhaps 10-15 years this technology could theoretically be used to capture and restore all CO_2 before its release into the atmosphere, as well as to generate hydrogen for vehicles powered by fuel cells. It should also help control emissions of mercury from power plants.
>
> This technology is called Integrated Gassicification Combined Cycle (IGCC). The biggest hurdle at present is high cost, and thus is not cost-effective.[24]

Given the above-mentioned technological breakthrough the present ecological crisis is not insurmountable theoretically. As we see, the major hurdle is the cost of implementation. The question is: Is the world too poor to finance the implementation of such new technologies? A brief look at the scenario of government's spending for defense worldwide would shed some light on the hidden side of political reality of the present world. The United States alone spends about 600 billion dollars for defense while there is virtually no major threat or enemy. More than this amount is spent by the European countries combined. The spending of Japan, China, India, Korea and Taiwan combined would come almost to this amount.[25] Several thousand billion dollars have been spent on defense worldwide while it

---

[26] Cf. *The Gaia Peace Atlas*, 216-224.

[27] Cf. Janet N. Abramovitz, "Taking a Stand: Cultivating a New Relationship with the World's forests," in *Worldwatch Paper* 140 (Washington, D. C.: Worldwatch Institute, 1998), 9-56; also see Alan Thein Durning, "Saving the Forests: What Will It Take," in *Worldwatch Paper* 117 (Washington, D. C.: Worldwatch Institute, 1993).

[28] Cf. Janet N. Abramovitz, "Taking a Stand," 9-16; also I. Colin Prentice, "Climate Change: Process and Production," in *Nature,* vol. 363 (May 20, 1993), 209.

is quite obvious that the world does not need that much weaponry in any way. This military spending logically spurs competition among nations for reason of national and psychological threat. Neighboring countries feel threatened by such large spending. To a certain extent arms production and military beef-up would create security and peace as demonstrated by the end of the cold war while at the same time this arms race placed a heavy burden upon many nations due to the ever more increased spending for defense. But the fact is that the world's political situation has changed much since the end of the cold war, and there exists no logical reason for countries to spend such huge amounts of money on defense. From an ecological point of view what we need and what the world needs most at present is not arms, weapons, and fighting, but love, fraternity, loving concern and respect among nations across the world.[26] There ought to exist a worldwide coordinated and concerted effort in addressing the problem. The Montreal Protocol is a good example in this case. Because of such coordinated and concerted effort worldwide in coping with the ozone-hole problem, as discussed above, the state of the ozone layer in the atmosphere has gradually recovered over the last few decades.

In short, nations ought to work more closely together by sharing material resources and technical know-how in coping with the problem. There is a need for a Special Fund to subsidize countries and corporations for the implementation of new technologies that fully reduce or capture emission of greenhouse gases. Developed countries ought to be willing to transfer the much needed technologies to developing countries so that such technologies would be applied widely to the effect of significantly reducing the greenhouse gases worldwide. There will be huge economic benefit for the rich and developed nations in return by sharing their

---

[29] The Amazon rainforest is considered as one of the planet's lungs along with the central Africa's rainforests. See Stuart Rice, "Saving Central Africa's Rainforests," in *New African*, No. 438 (March 2005), 38.

[30] Claudio Angelo, "Punctuated Disequilibriums Occasional but Extreme Climate Could Turn Parts of the Amazon Rain Forest into Dry Savanna," in *Scientific American*, vol. 292, No. 2 (February 2005), 12.

[31] Cf. Hans Schwarz, *Creation*, 179-183.

[32] Per Larsson, *Thy Will Be Done on Earth*, 48f.

resources and technologies with developing countries because the latter will develop technologically and economically more rapidly by applying such technologies while minimizing significantly economic losses through ecological crisis. As Janet N. Abramovitz has discussed about the importance of forests and the need for good management of forests,[27] ecological crisis would become less and also easier to be tackled if nations worked together in reforestation of the earth's surface. The effectiveness of forests in regulating the climate is well recognized.[28] Recently the *Scientific American* made again the alarming report that the Amazon natural black forest in Brazil is being steadily deforested by reckless commercial logging.[29] If this trend continues for a few more years, the Amazon forest can become a savanna in the not too-distant future.[30] At present scientists cannot calculate exactly how extensive the possible ecological consequences will be. Rich and developed nations ought to help the poor developing countries both with the needed technical know-how and financial support so that the reforestation of the earth could proceed at a speed needed for bringing the climate problem under control before it becomes uncontrollable. All this shows that the role human beings can play in the whole of nature's ecosystem is really important, and this makes us aware of our role as co-workers of God in the continuation of divine creative activities in the world.

6.3 Human Beings as Co-workers

In considering the importance of human beings as co-workers of God we would need first to remind ourselves of the theological implication of the creation of human beings in the image of God. Theologically, human creation in the image of God can be seen and interpreted to imply that human beings are the representatives of God here on earth, and thus ought to be co-workers of God.[31] In view of the eminent role which human beings

---

[33] For more about Moltmann's view on this point see his *God in Creation: An Ecological Doctrine of Creation*, trans., Margaret Kohl (London: SCM Press, 1985).

[34] Cf. Jürgen Moltmann, "The Ecological Crisis: Peace with Nature," in *Scottish Journal of Religious Studies* 9 (1988), 7f.

[35] Cf. Salai Hla Aung, *The Doctrine of Creation in the Theology of Barth, Moltmann and Pannenberg*, 108-110.

play in the wellbeing of nature's ecosystem we can argue that God has created the world, and has left to human beings the task of keeping His creation in good health through the caring, nurturing and protecting of other fellow beings and nature as well.[32] Here we ought to ask ourselves the question whether or not we are fulfilling this God-given obligation in our relation with others and the surrounding nature. Unless we ask this question ourselves and take our obligation toward nature seriously, nature will never be renewed and resuscitated. When nature is not renewed and resuscitated it will not be good for us human beings either since our fate and fortune is basically related to nature through the bound of the ecosystem.

In reality, however, we see that our understanding of human creation in divine image and our disposition thereof are a bit different from what we ought to be by this theologically if seen and interpreted from an ecological point of view. Jürgen Moltmann is right when he argues that we have narrowly understood and interpreted the human creation in the image of God. In Moltmann's view the human creation in the image of God is usually interpreted anthropocentrically.[33] That is to say, human beings are the highest species among all the earthly creatures, and thus are superior to all other creatures and hold a special privilege of lordship over them just as God is Lord over the whole creation as naturally warranted by His Creatorship.[34] In that way the human creation in the image of God becomes a warrant for lordship over nature and all earthlings. On the other hand, the conceptual input that gives rise to this sort of anthropocentric understanding and interpretation of human creation in the image of God is the theological exposition of the idea. Theologically interpreted, human beings are human only when they do actually conquer nature and have a control over it in the same manner as God holds a Lordship over the whole creation.[35] This paves the way for human beings to set themselves against nature, and at the same time try their best to conquer nature so that they may become true to the very motif of their being created in the image of God. Conceptually we can call this theological orientation as an understanding and interpretation of divine creation exclusively in a masculine sense. That is, the creaturehood of human beings and their relation to the surrounding nature are to be understood and

---

[36] Per Larsson, *Your Will Be Done on Earth*, 134.

interpreted exclusively in terms of might, power, authority, oppression, exploitation, and so on.

Conceptually interpreted, the understanding and interpretation of divine creation exclusively in a masculine sense apparently stands in direct contradiction to the very nature of God's own being. In our discussion about the relationship among the three persons of the Godhead we note that the fount of God's being lies in the mutually beneficial and symbiotic relationship of the three persons of the Godhead. We also note that this relationship is the very source of the continuation of life in God's being. In fact, there can be a continuation of life even when there is no reciprocal and responsible relationship between human beings and their surrounding nature. But the continuation of life in this way will not be lasting and enjoyable simply because of the creation of imbalances through such relationship. Our consideration of nature's ecosystem shows that the capacity of nature's ecosystem has a limit to bear imbalances within its own life. Moreover, the understanding and interpretation of divine creation exclusively in a masculine sense would not also be helpful in restoring the broken covenant between God and human beings, between human beings, and also between human beings and nature. Instead, it will only intensify the consequence of the broken covenant through the spirit of Babel spawn by our desire to become like God through our scientific achievements. The spirit of Babel will further lead us away from God, thereby minimizing the chances for the renewal and resuscitation of nature by establishing a new covenantal relationship. The following statement of the Christian Conference of Asia (CCA) Environmental Training Workshop held in Saitama, Japan, in 2002 will help us see the spirit of Babel and its ecological implication and significance:

> After people shared their experiences and mentioned their environmental situation, we recognized our frailties as stewards. We destroyed His image in us because we wanted to be like God (the fall) and built things to glorify ourselves as humans (Tower of Babel). We have disrupted the systems and cycles of nature as designed perfectly by God because we thought that we are better than God. We alienated ourselves from Him and from creation because we put ourselves in His place.[36]

Whether the understanding and interpretation of divine creation exclusively in a masculine sense is a right one is difficult to judge. One thing we should not overlook but take seriously in our interpretation of the theological implication of divine creation is the feminine element in the creation account. In the creation story we read that having created the rest of creatures God summons Adam to himself and asks him to name them all. This is often interpreted as God's warrant to human beings for dominion over all other creatures. As discussed above, this is simply a good example of masculine understanding and interpretation. If seen and interpreted from another angle, the text can mean quite the opposite. Naming other and establishing a relation with others through calling the other's name are not, in a strict analysis, the way to dominion and self-exaltation over against others. Logically speaking, what lies behind the giving of a name to another is a feeling of affinity, kinship, and close relationship. We never ask our enemy to name our newly-born babies. The same is true with the establishment of relation with others by calling their name. We never call our enemies by their name in a sweet and soft tone. Even when we do, we then usually call their name in a harsh tone in order to convey the message to them that we are not their friends. In view of all this God's asking of human being to name other creatures cannot be seen and interpreted as a divine warrant to humans for dominion over them but His invitation and instruction to human beings to establish and enter into a close and friendly relationship with them. Conceptually we can call this theological orientation as an understanding and interpretation of divine creation exclusively in a feminine sense. That is, the creaturehood of human beings and their relation to the surrounding nature are to be seen and interpreted exclusively in terms of affinity, kindness, sympathy, pity, care, concern, protection and so on.

Seeing and interpreting divine creation in a feminine sense will help much in restoring the broken covenant because it will generate and nurture mutual love and respect. We have noted earlier that there is life when there is relationship. This is so because relationship generates and nurtures mutual understanding, love and respect. It is interesting to note that even God lowers and empties himself taking on the form of a human being in order to establish relationship with us. By entering into a relationship with us God is able to restore the covenant that had been broken. We can also note that the kind of relationship God has chosen is a self-denial and other-centered kind of relationship (Phil. 2:6-11). This self-denial and other-centeredness has enabled God to restore the covenant that had already been broken. This is the inner spirituality of the new covenant. The lesson we can learn from the inner spirituality of this new covenant with regard to ecological realities in our life environment is that we must imitate God's way in restoring our broken relationship with others and nature. That means we need to lower and empty ourselves and enter into a respectful and grateful relationship with others and nature if we really mean to heal the wounds of our past relationship with others and nature. In that way we may be able to restore our broken covenant with others and nature so that others and nature will be renewed and resuscitated both physically and ecologically.

This is also the very challenge of our spiritual commitment and also the very task to which we are called by God. This is also the main challenge and responsibility of our Christian service and stewardship. In Lutheran theology we note the importance and centrality of the concept of vocation with regard to our spiritual life. Vocation is a spiritual service which we fulfill as part of our Christian duty in direct personal relationship to God. Vocation in Martin Luther's view is not confined to services in the Church only, but includes preserving God's creation as well as rendering good services to the government, society, and fellow human beings. By caring for God's creation we participate in and continue the creation work of God as his co-workers. Here we ought to remind ourselves of the stewardship to which we are called by God. We are called by God to tend and keep his creation. We remember that the purpose of God's incarnation in human form is to establish a new covenant, i.e., his kingdom of love, justice and equality, by renewing the fallen creation. Humans being created in the image of God and God's incarnation in the form of a human being clearly testify that human beings are the immediate covenant partner of God. This, however, should not be stressed in order to exclude the extra-human creation in the newly covenanted life which is established through the life, death and resurrection of Jesus. The scope of the new covenant is to be extended in order to bring into its sphere the extra-human creation.

As pointed out above, the extra-human creation is never lost sight of in the covenant of God with human beings. This is evident in God's covenant with Adam and Noah. It is also evident in Mk. 16:15 where we see Jesus saying to his disciples "Go into all the world and preach the good news to all creation." The phrase "all creation" clearly points to the